Adult Feathers coloring book

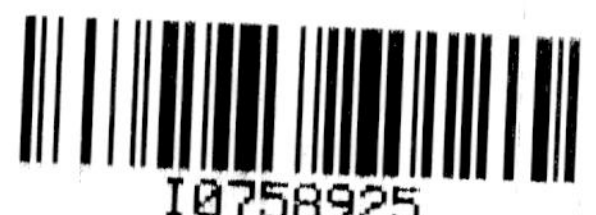

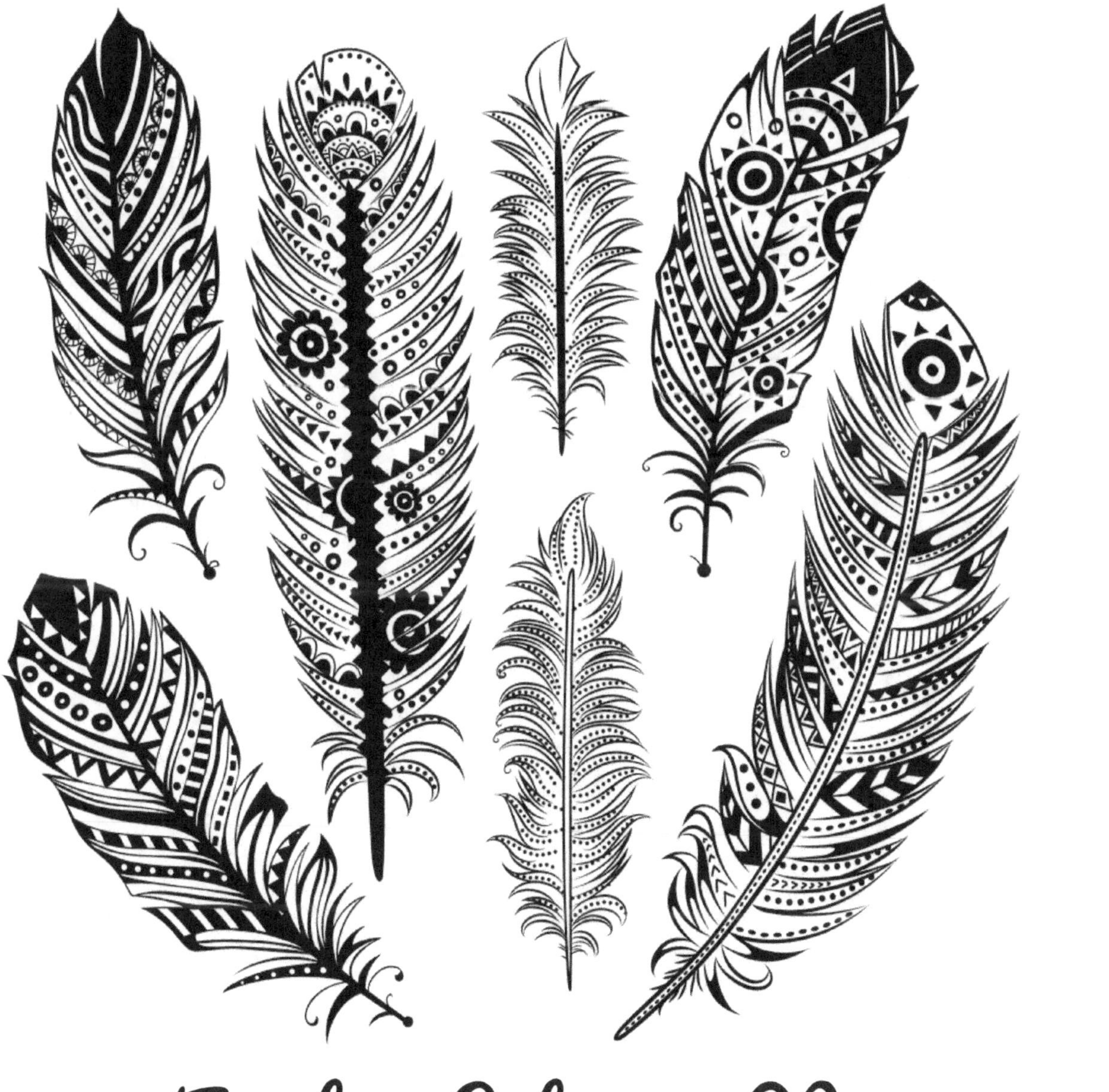

52 Feather Coloring Pages

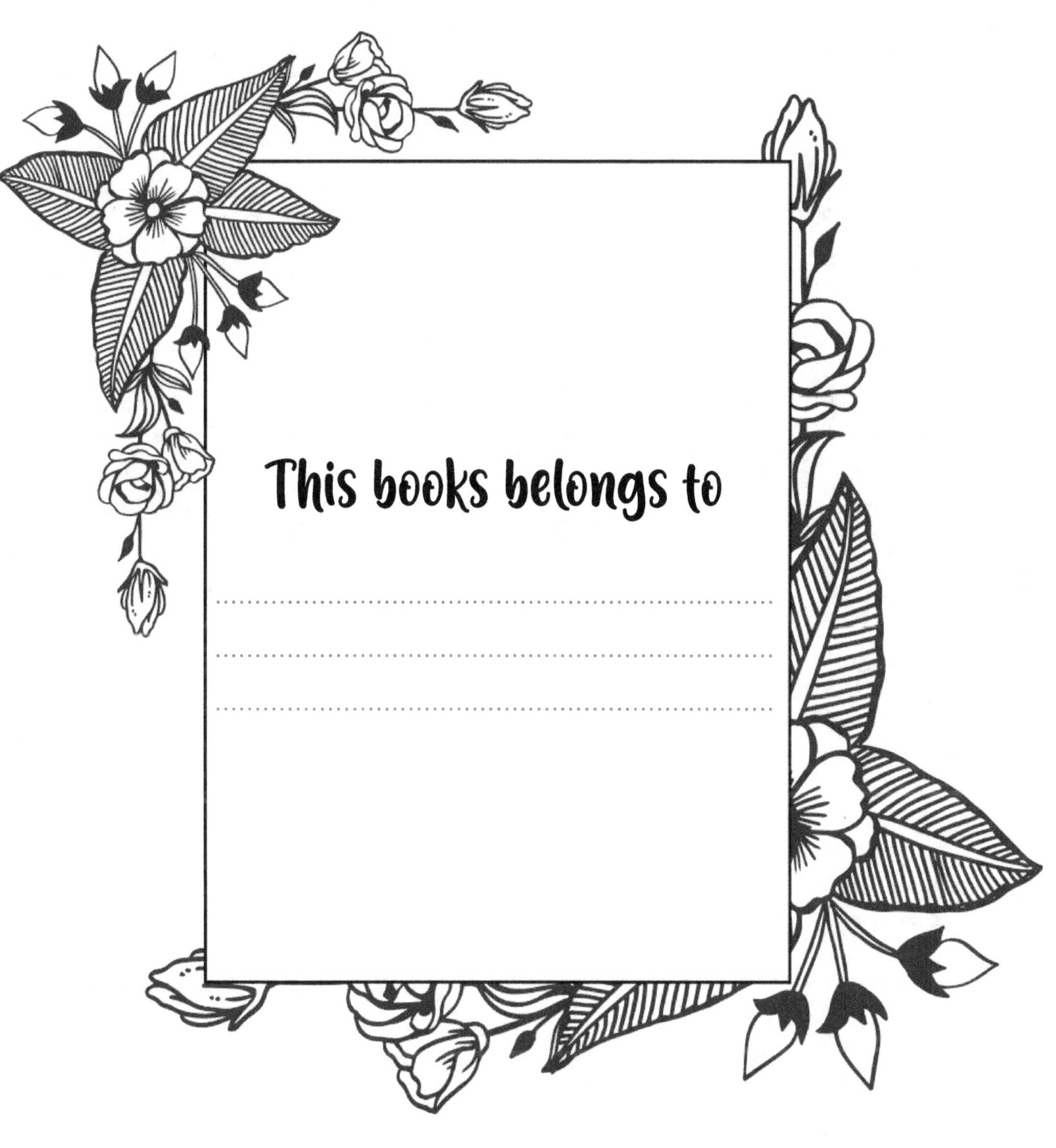

This books belongs to

Color Test Page

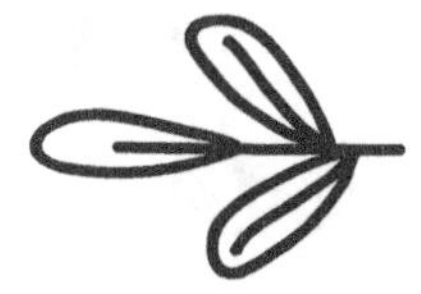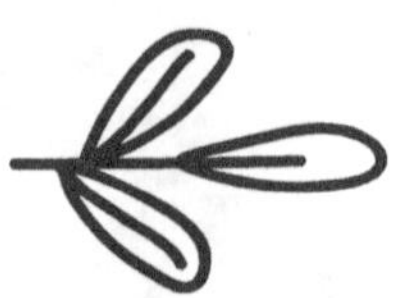

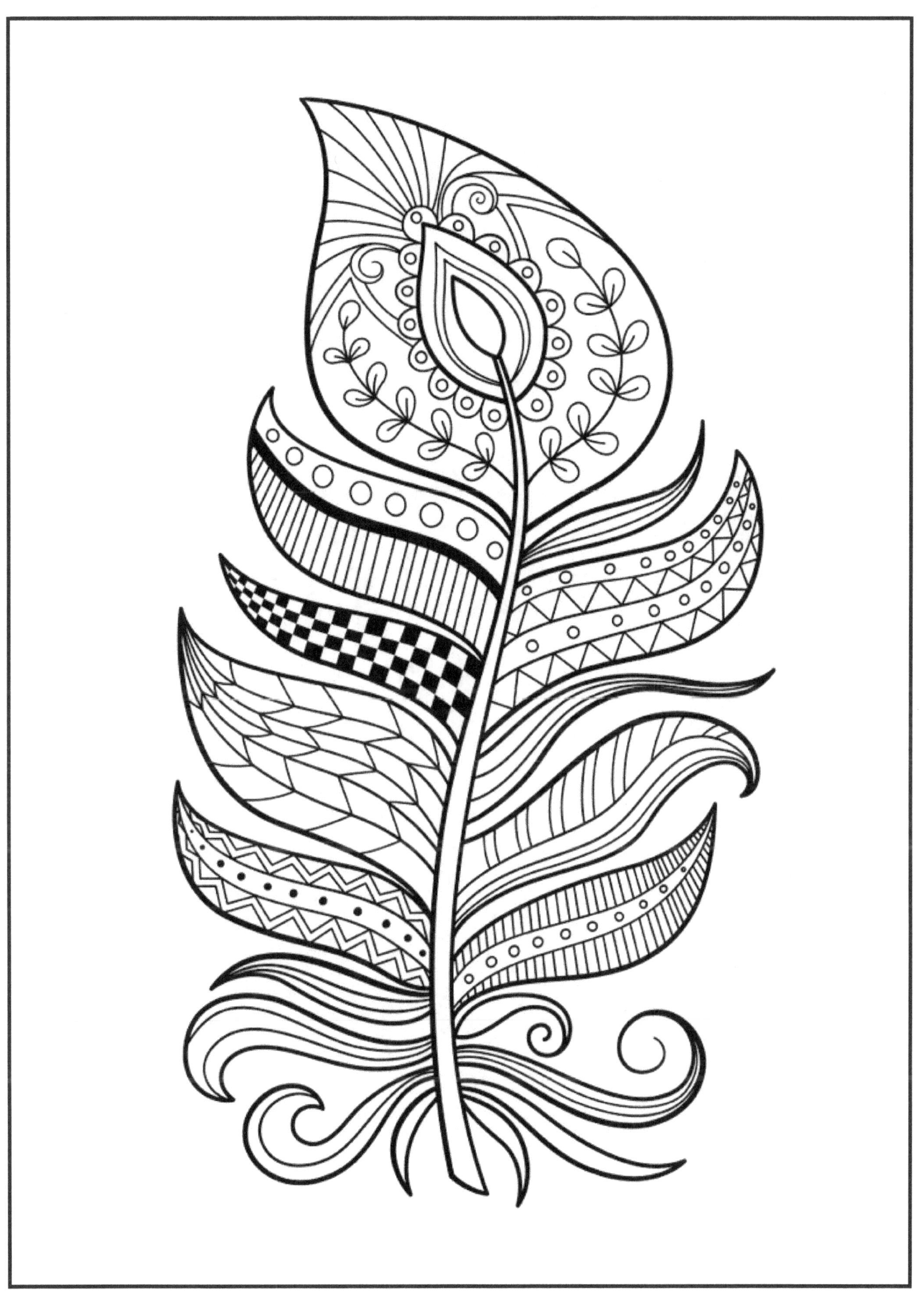

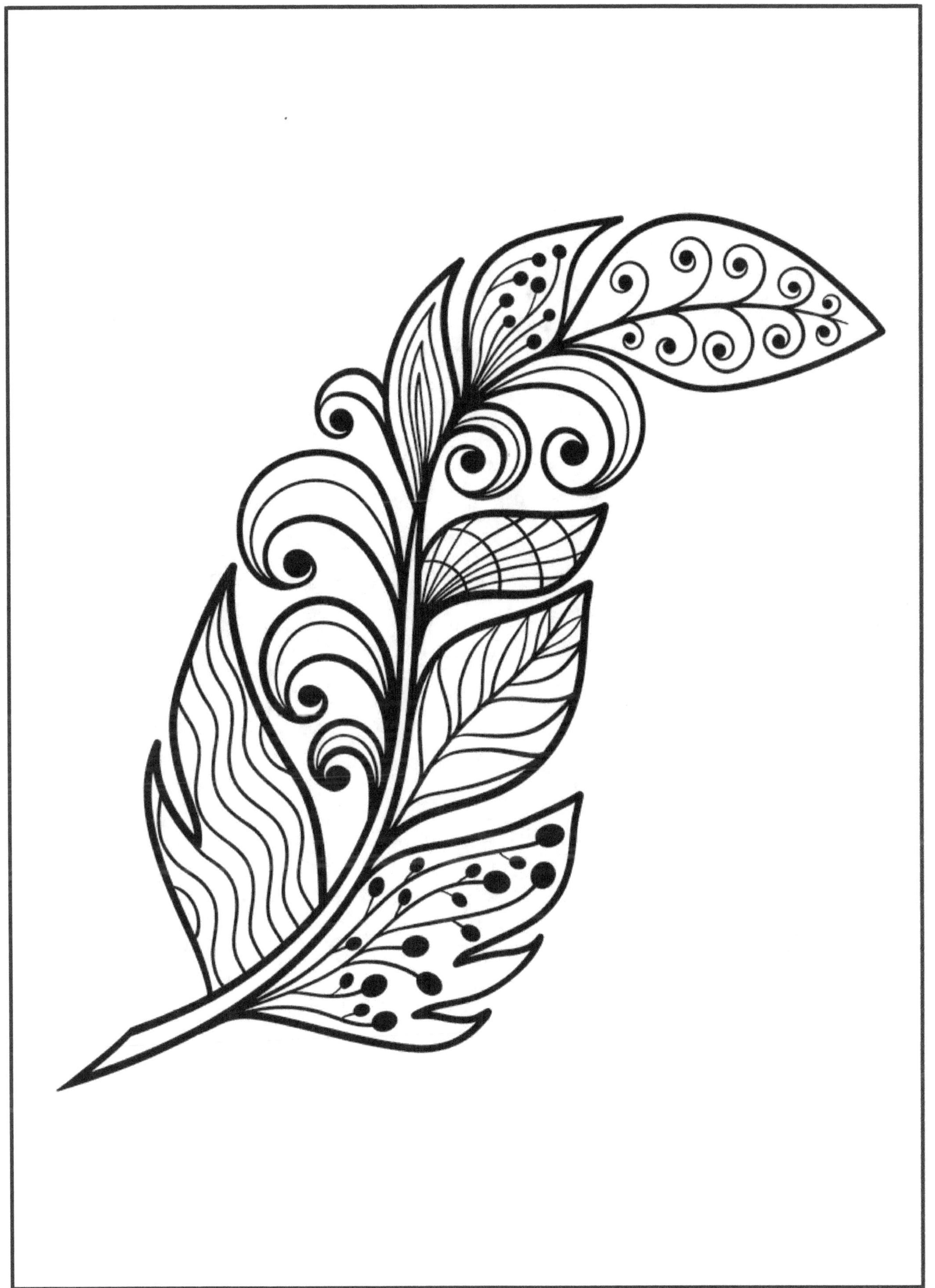

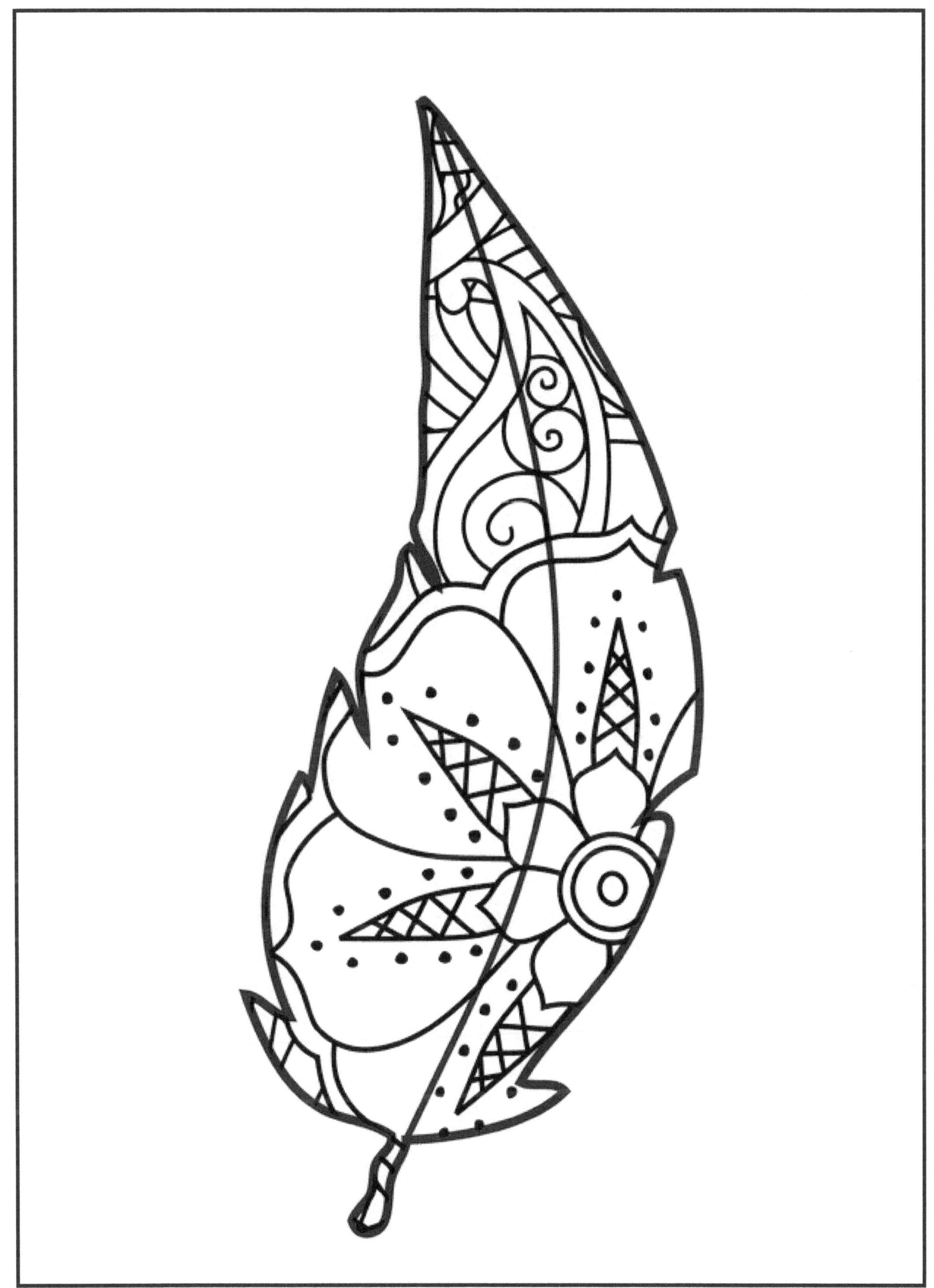

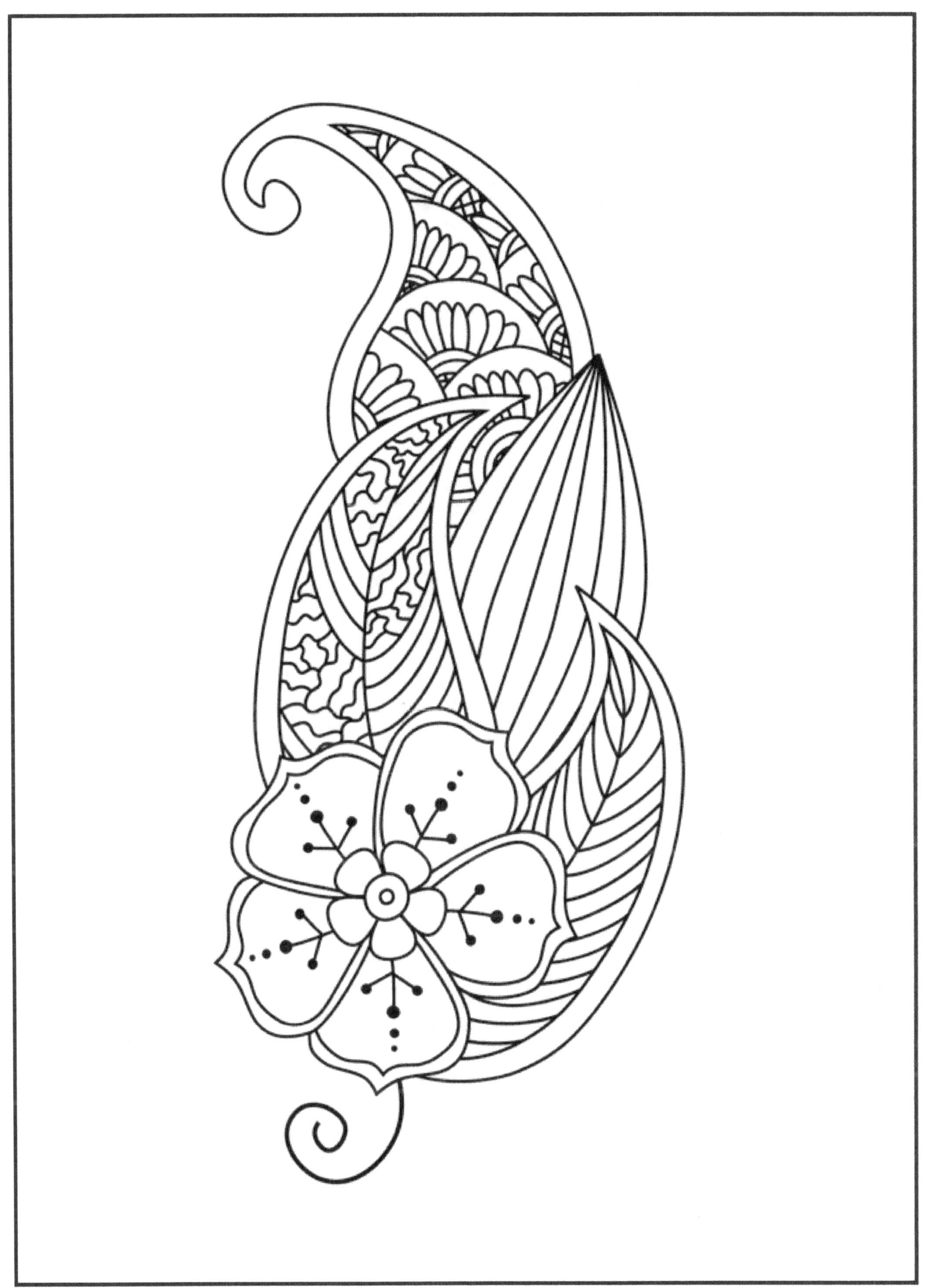

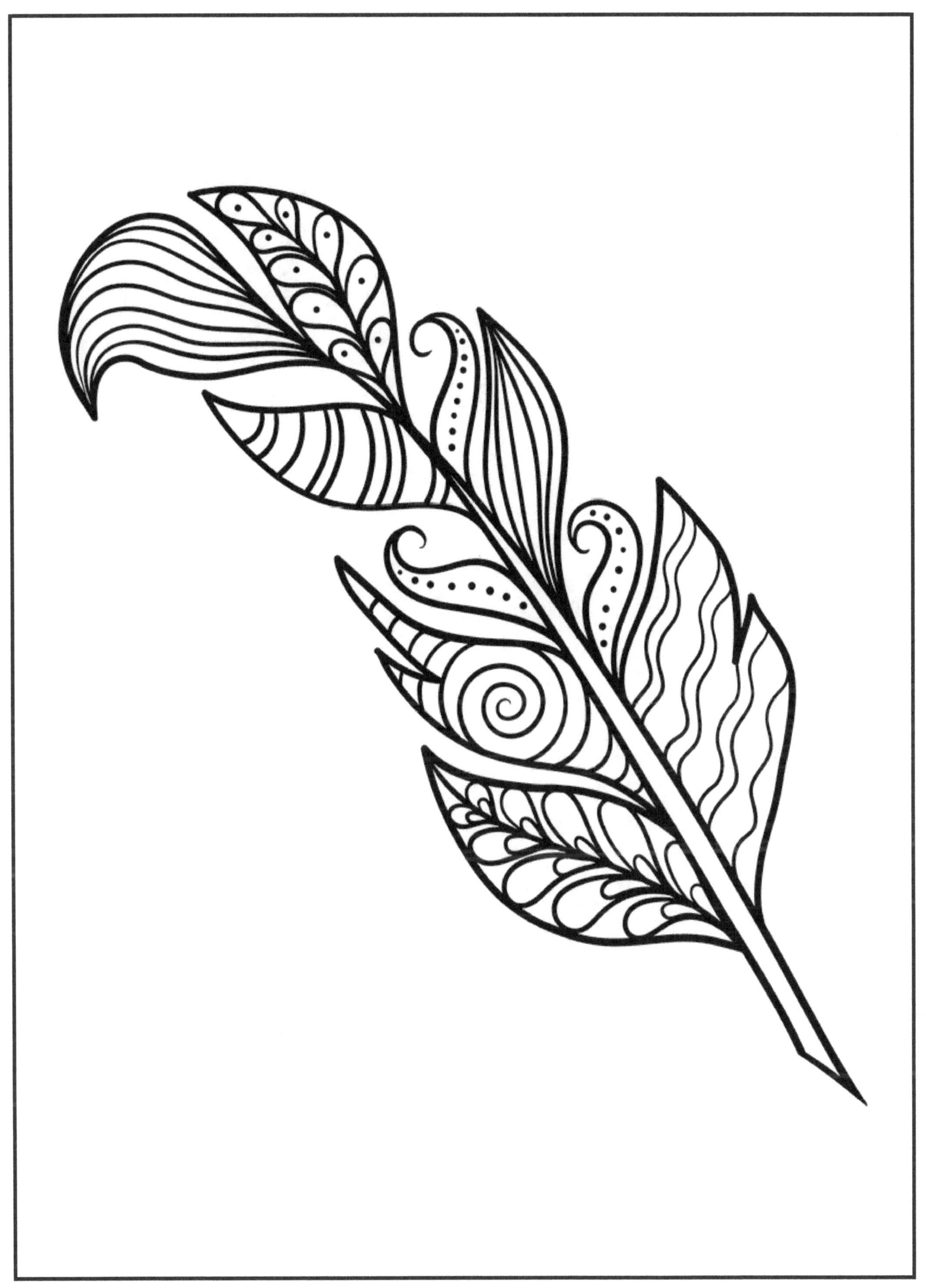

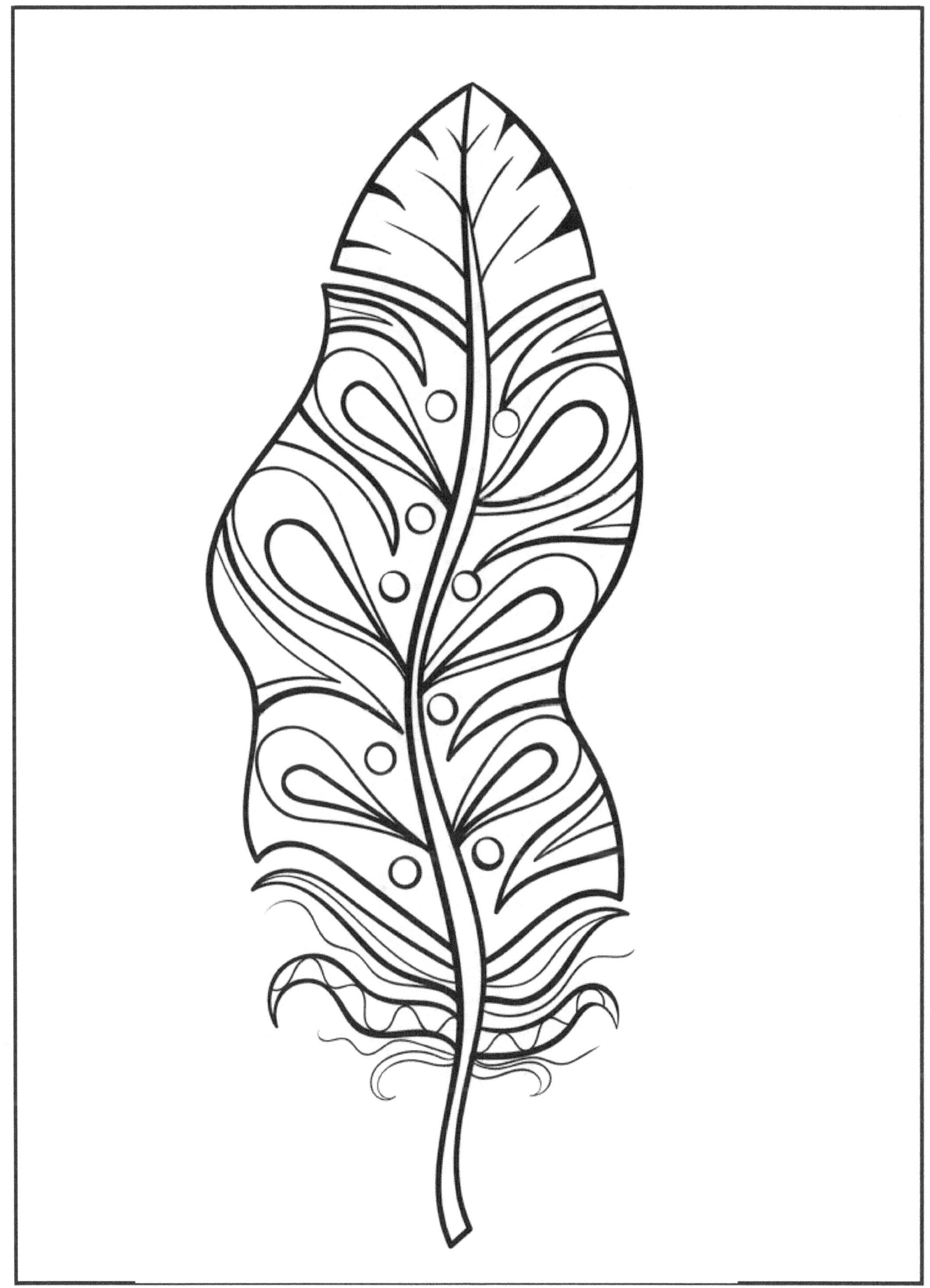

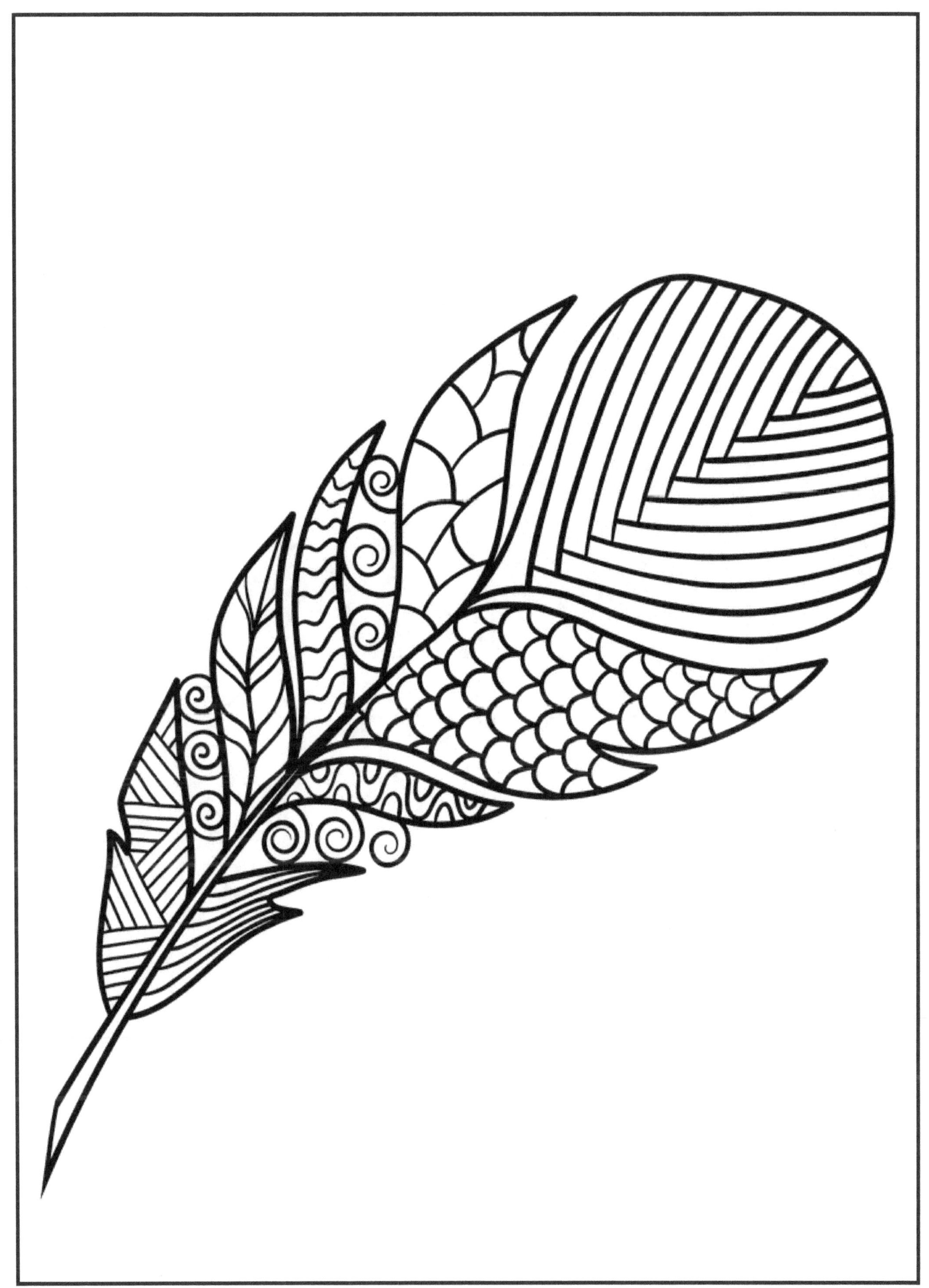

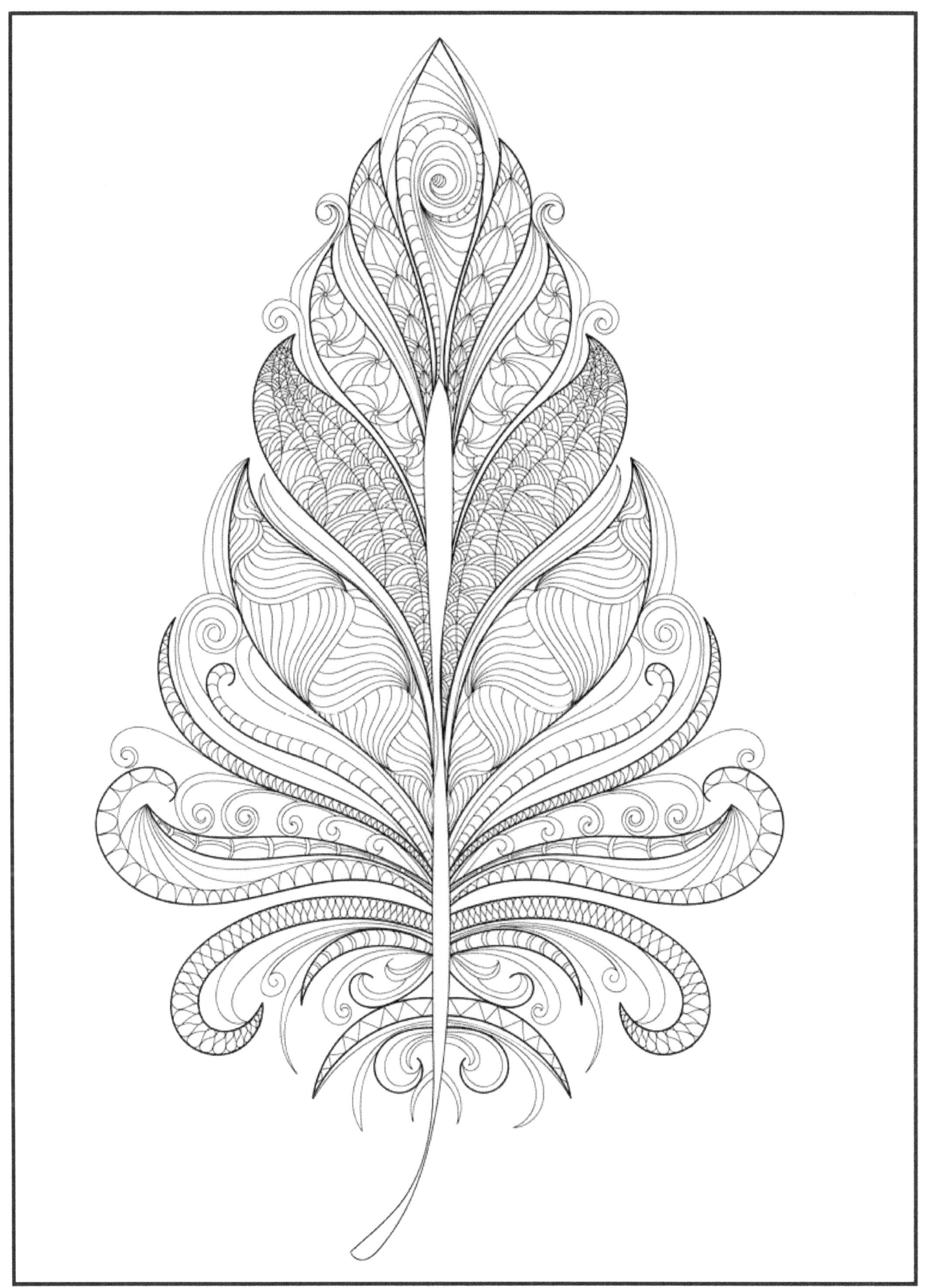

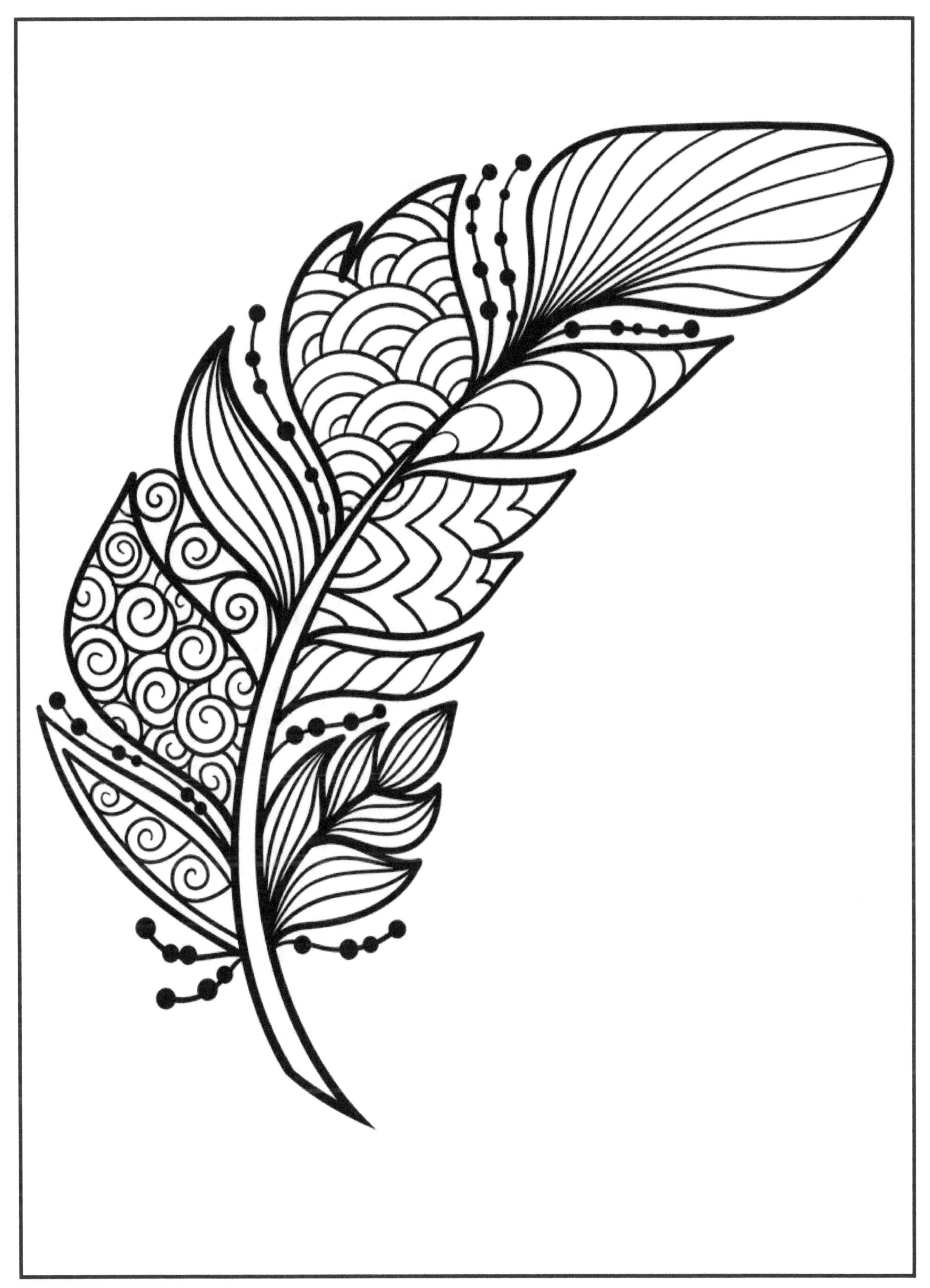

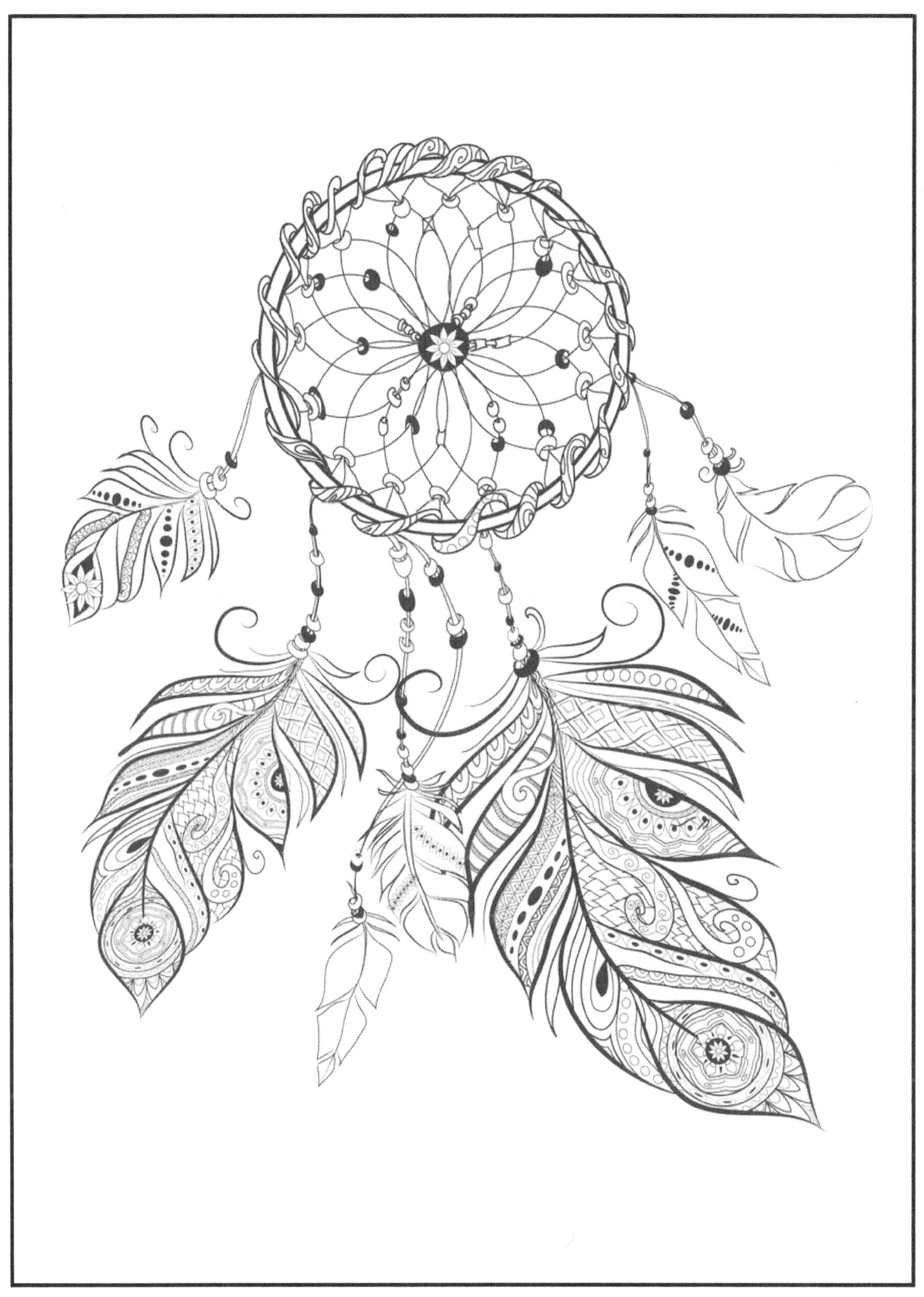

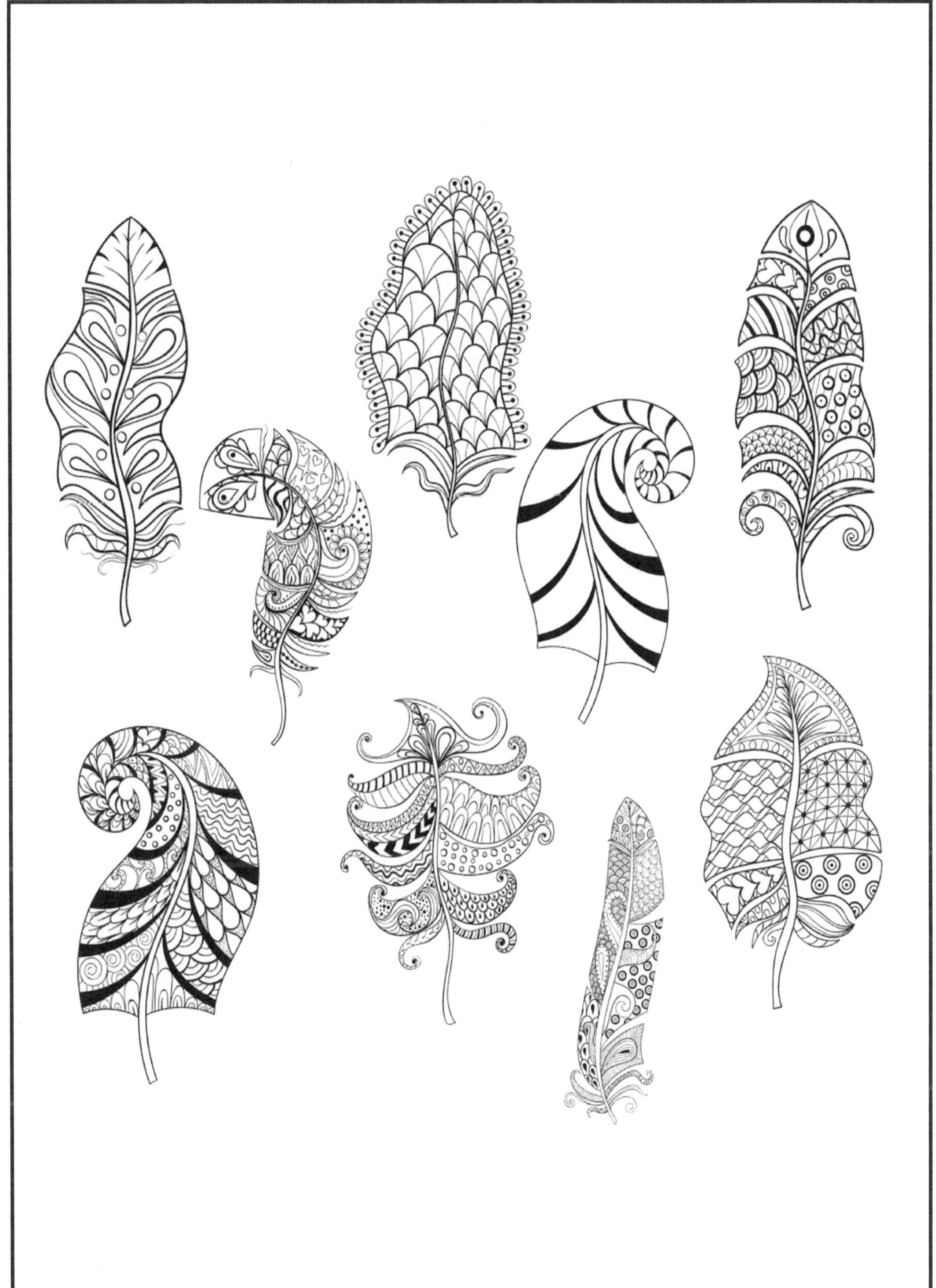

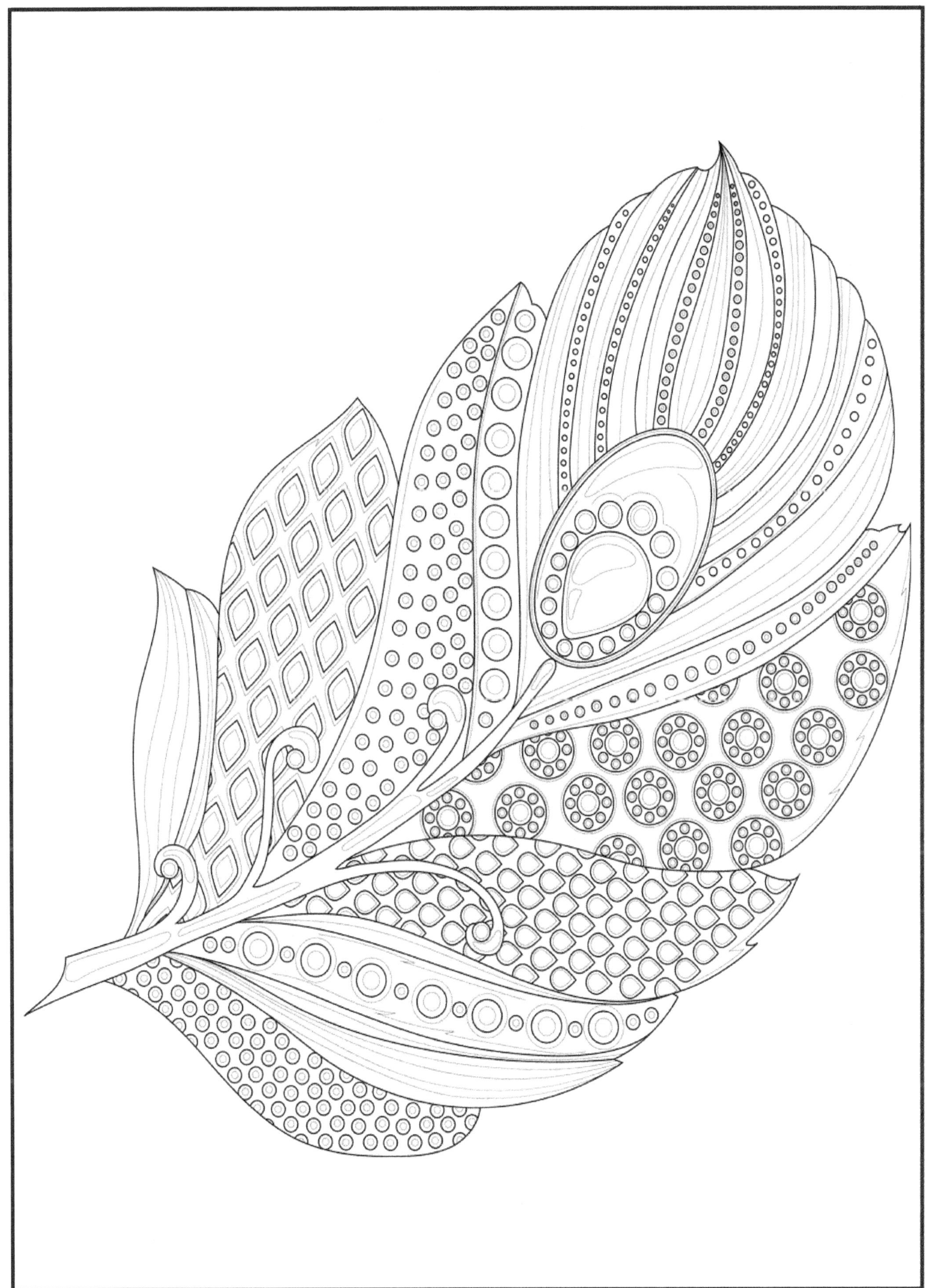

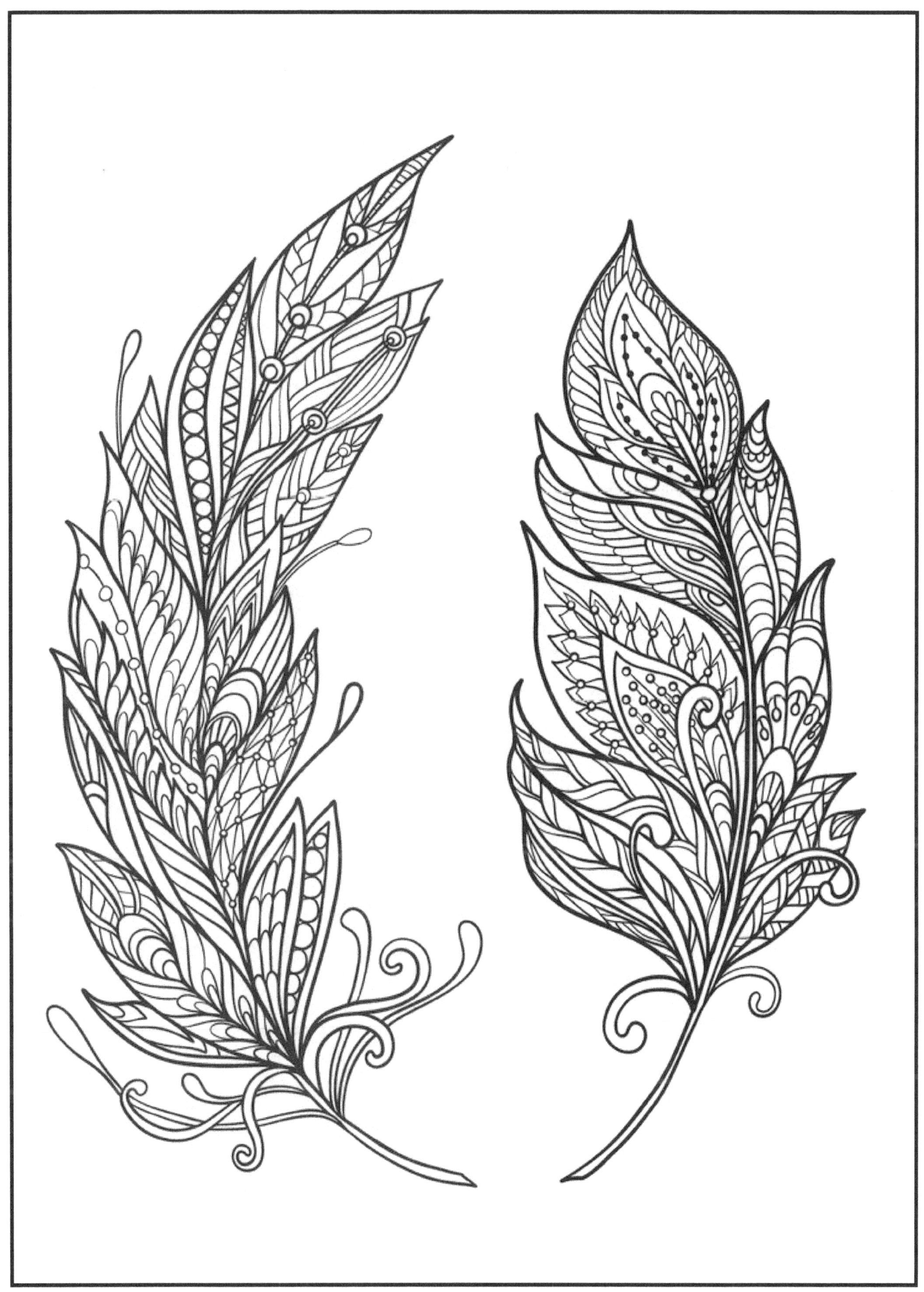

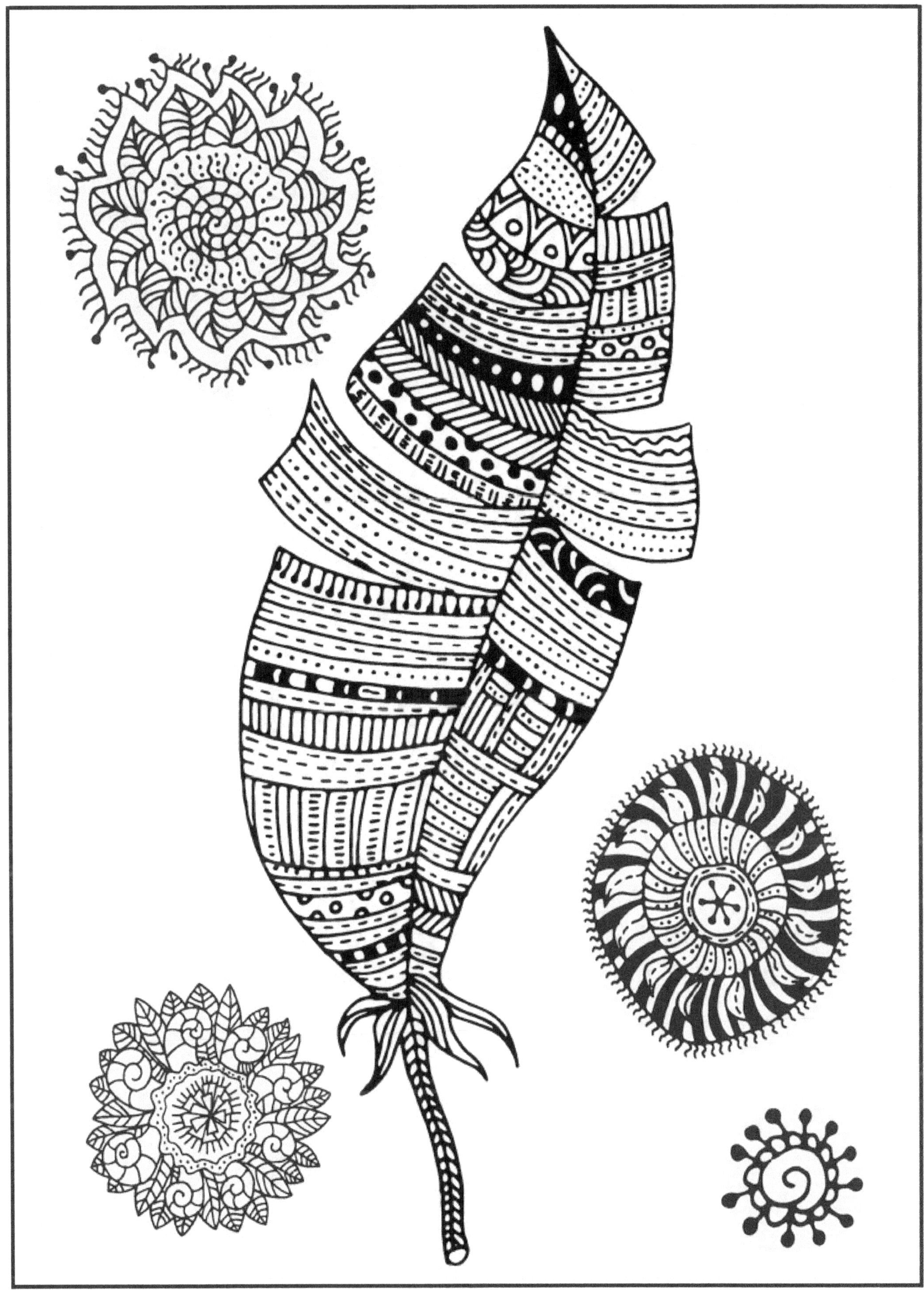

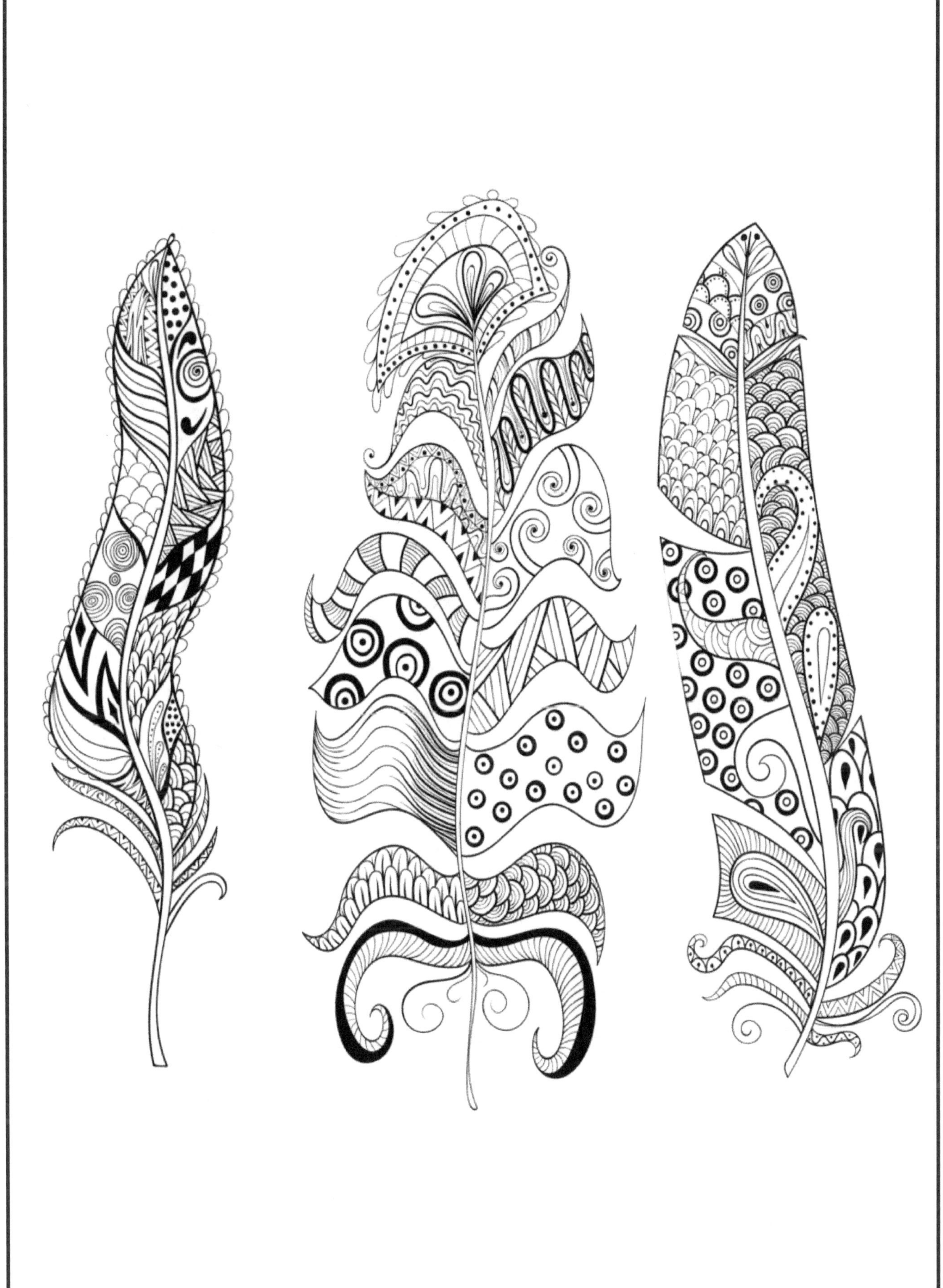

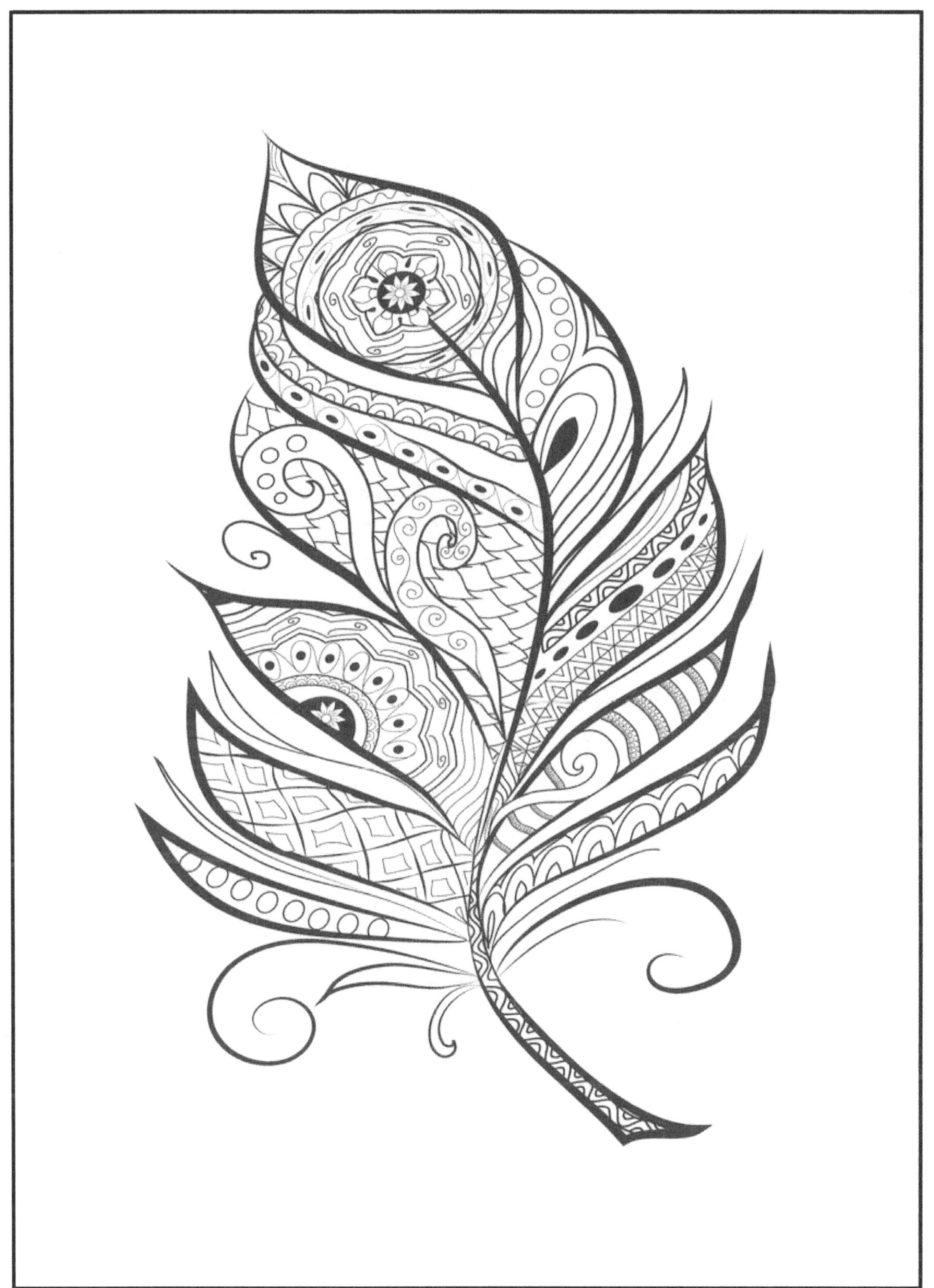

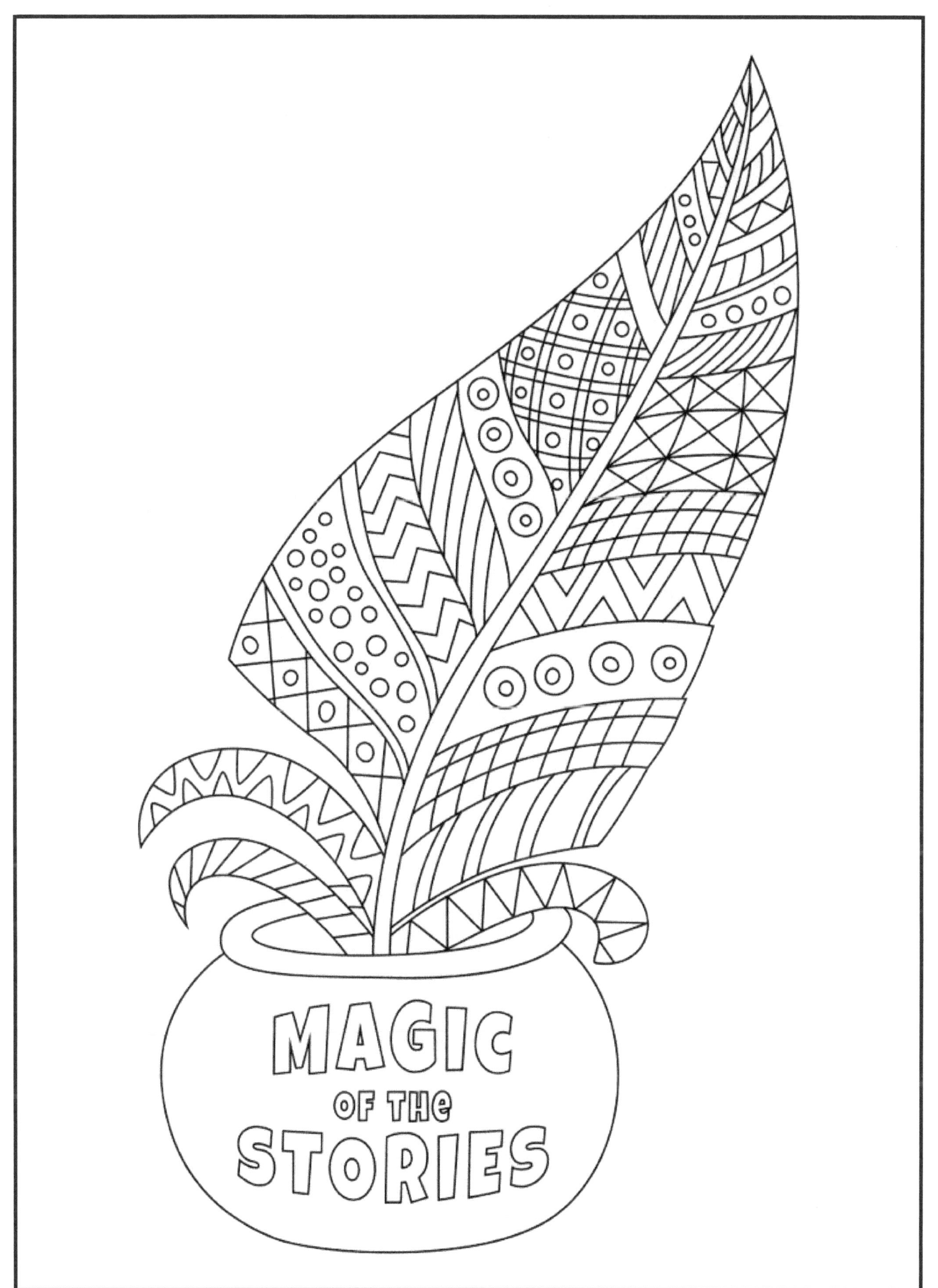

MAGIC
OF THE
STORIES

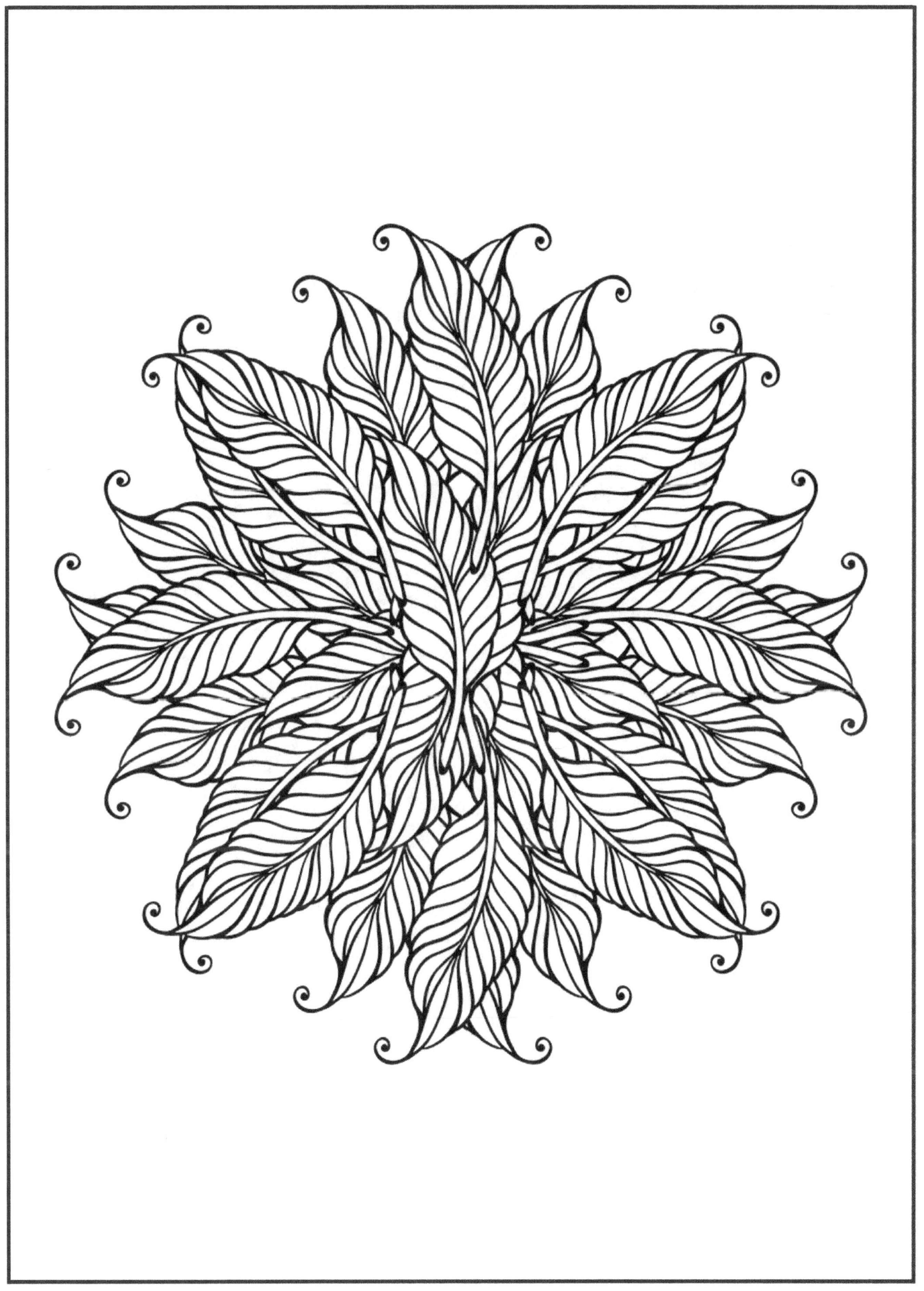

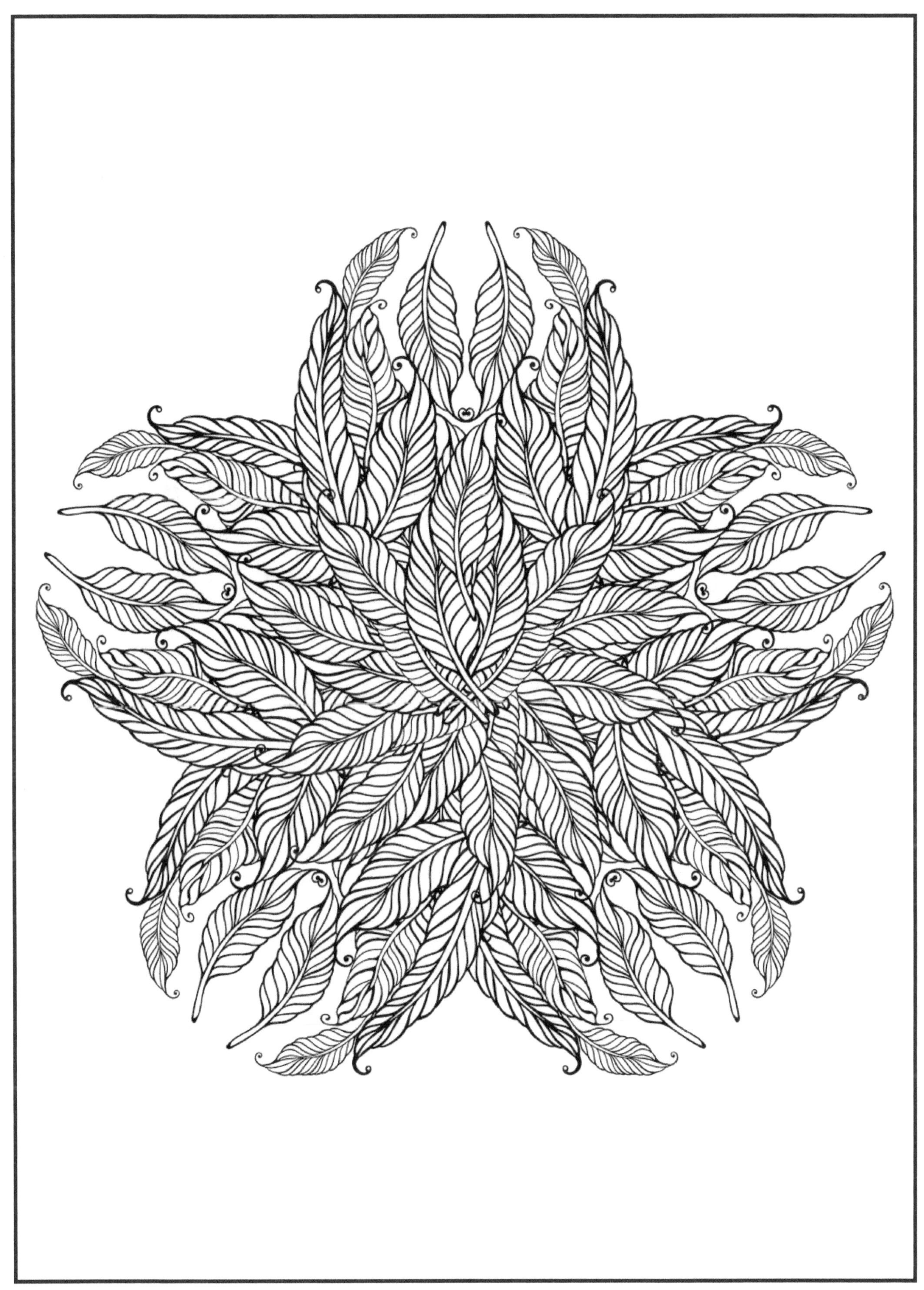

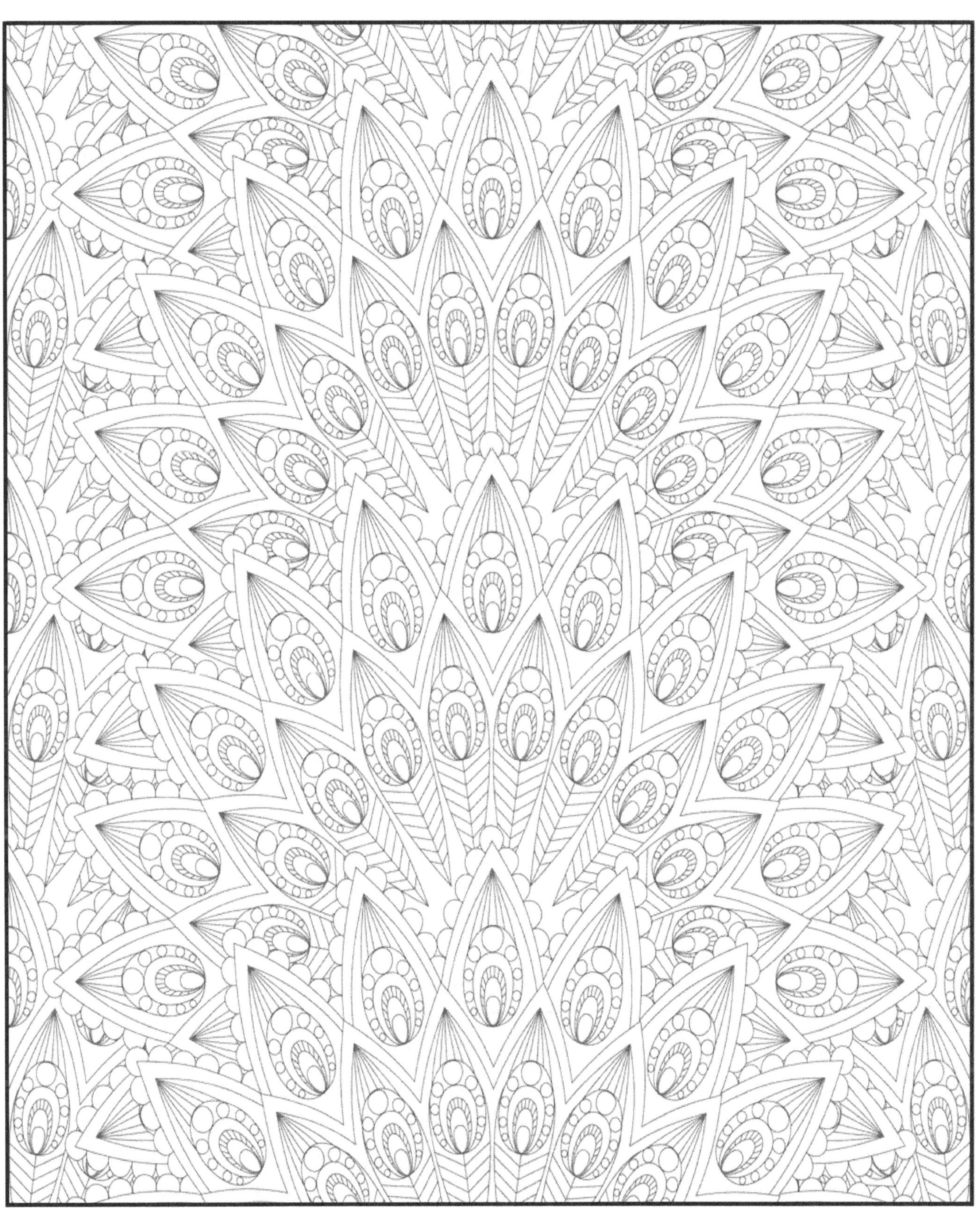

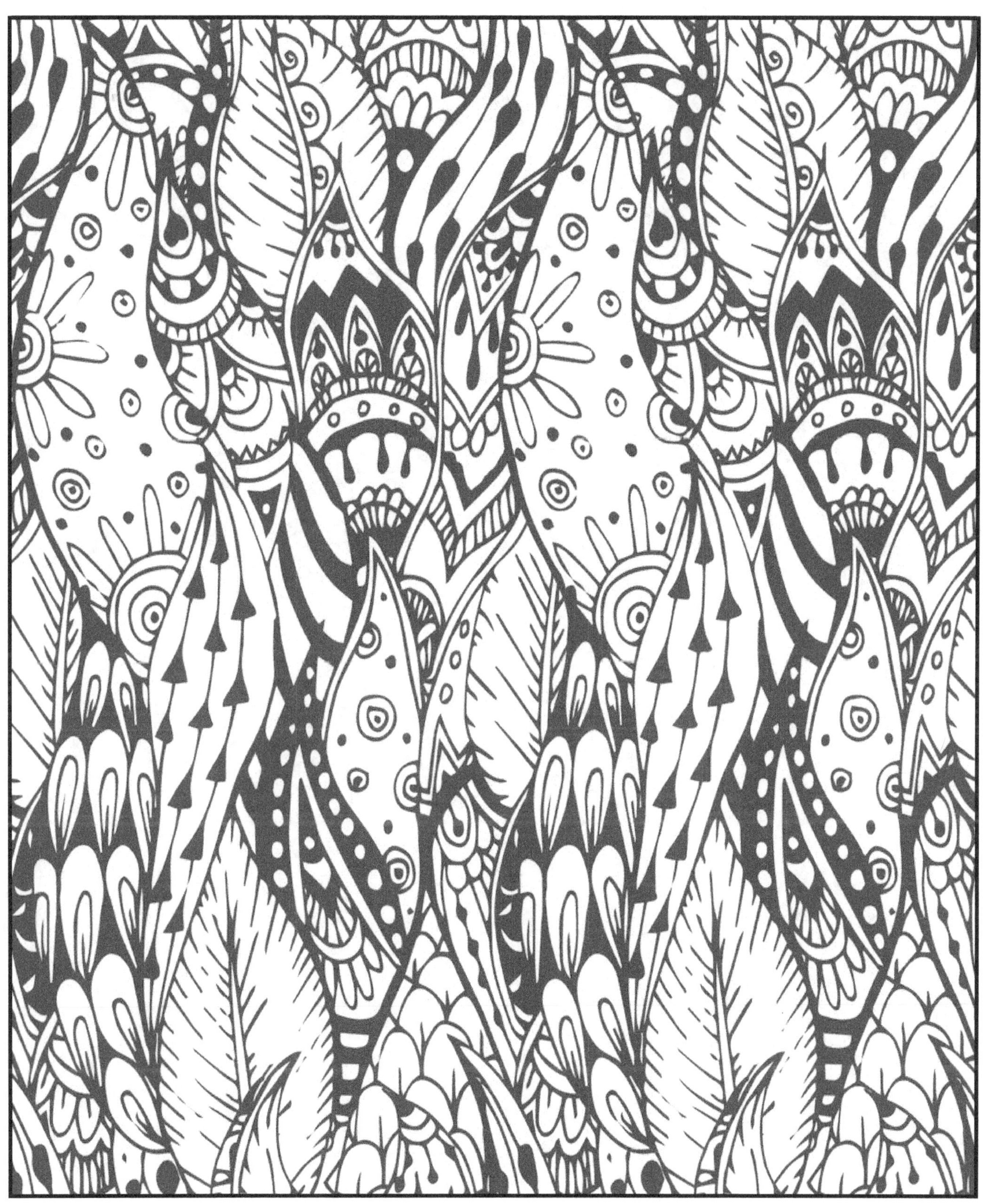

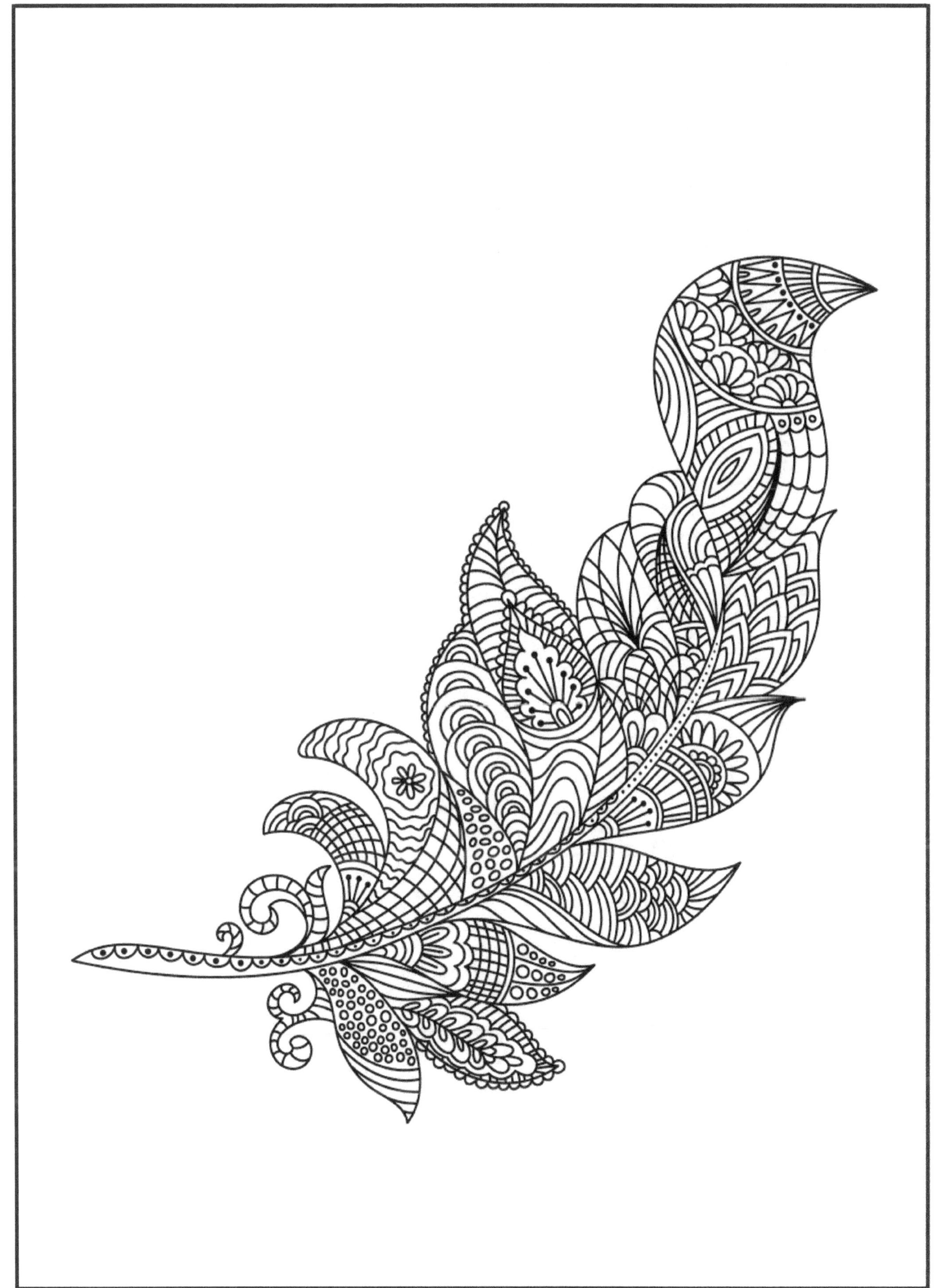

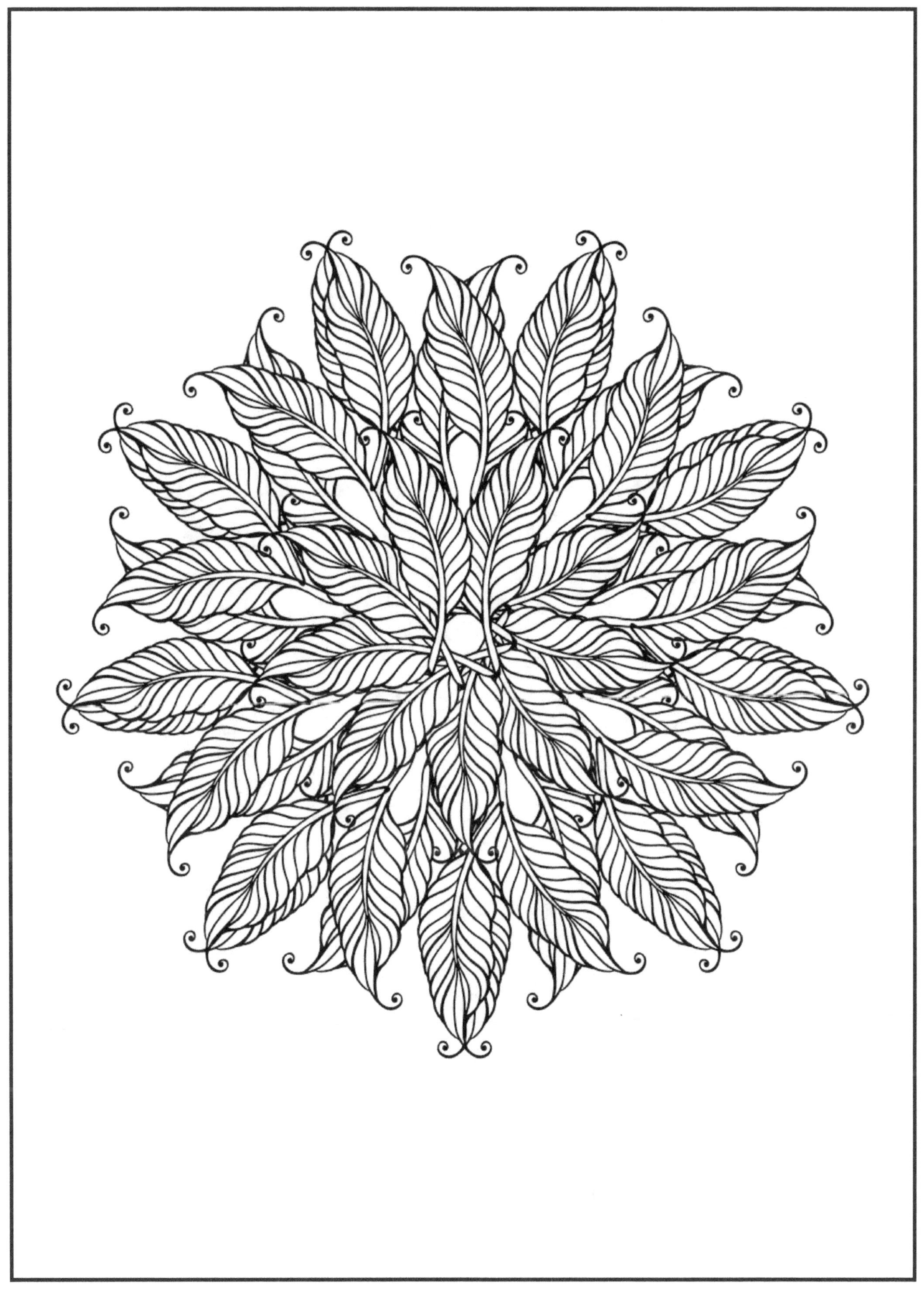

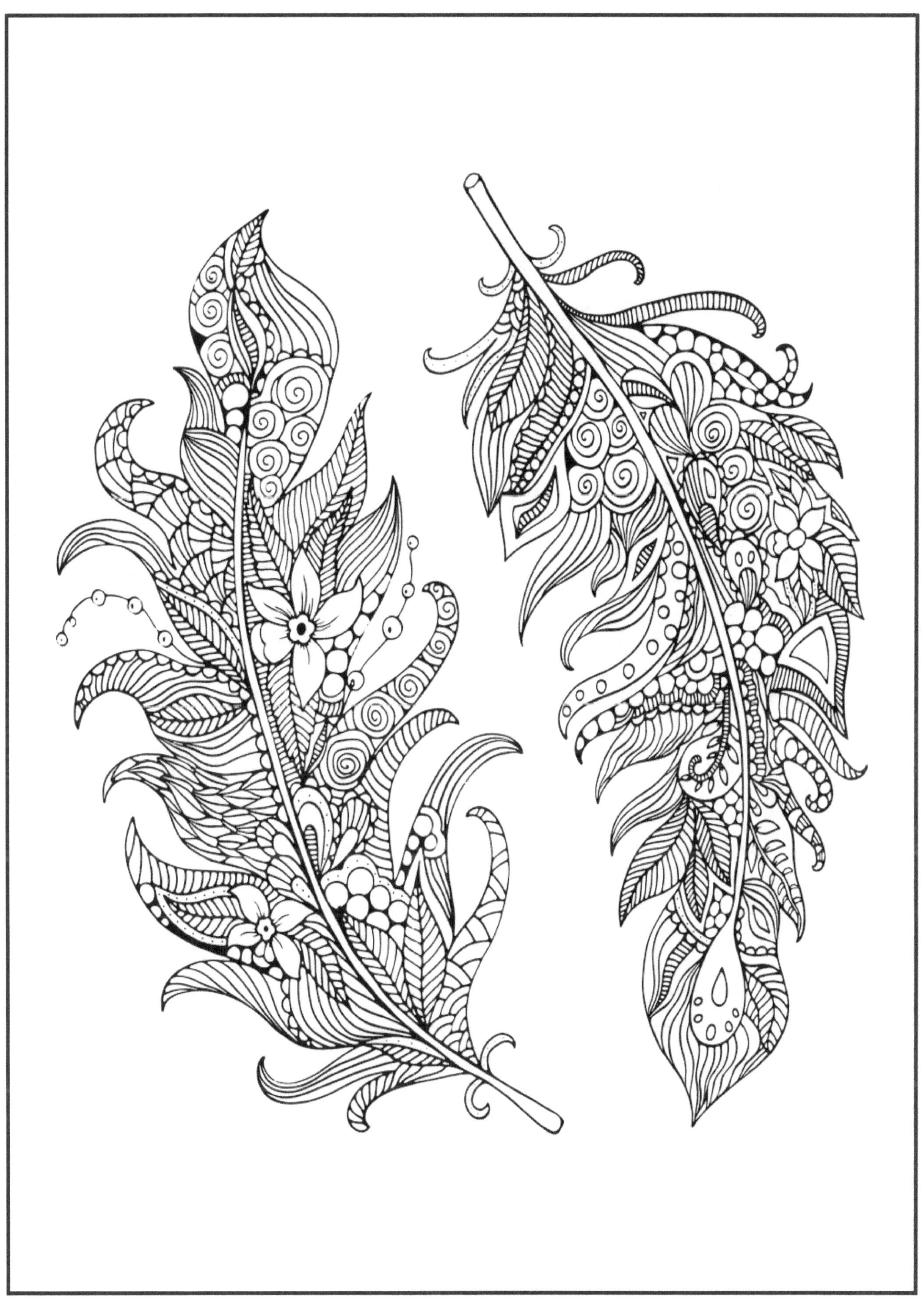

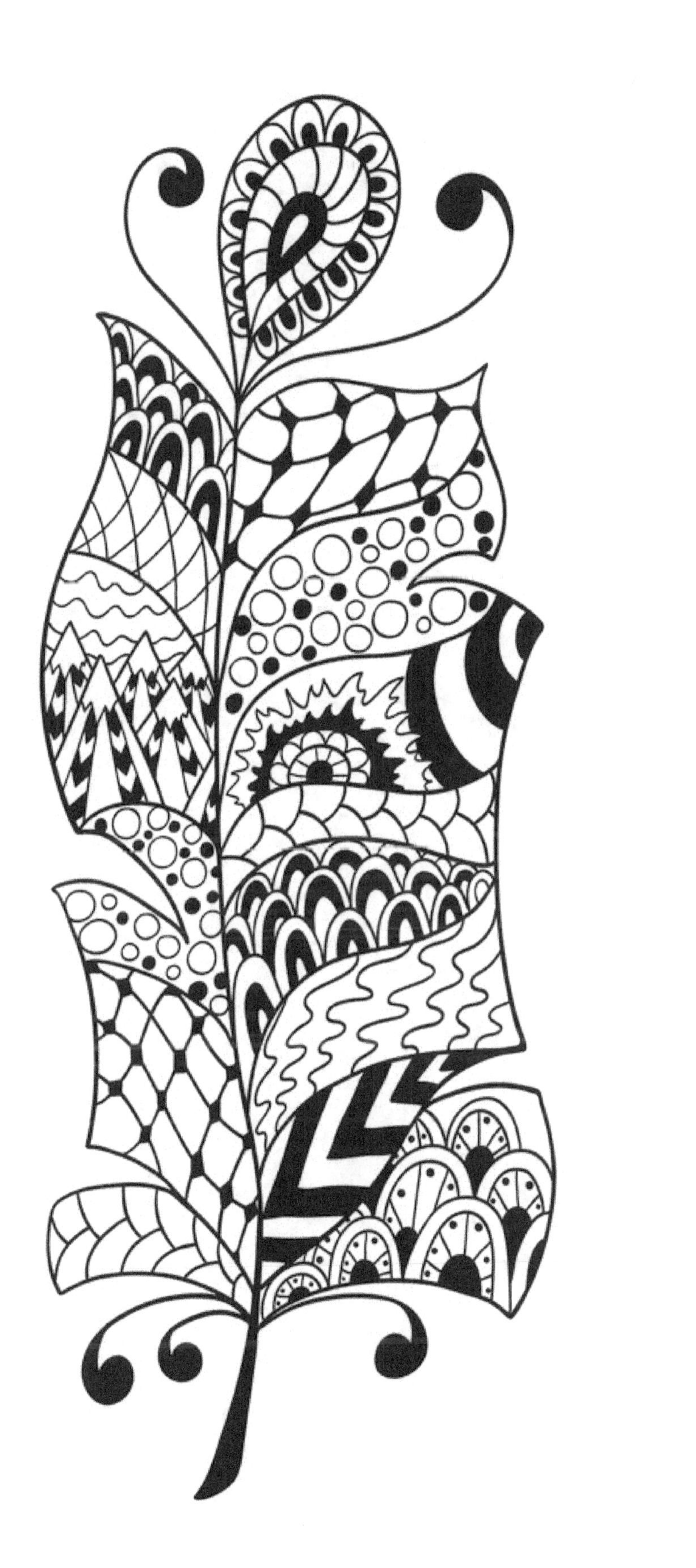

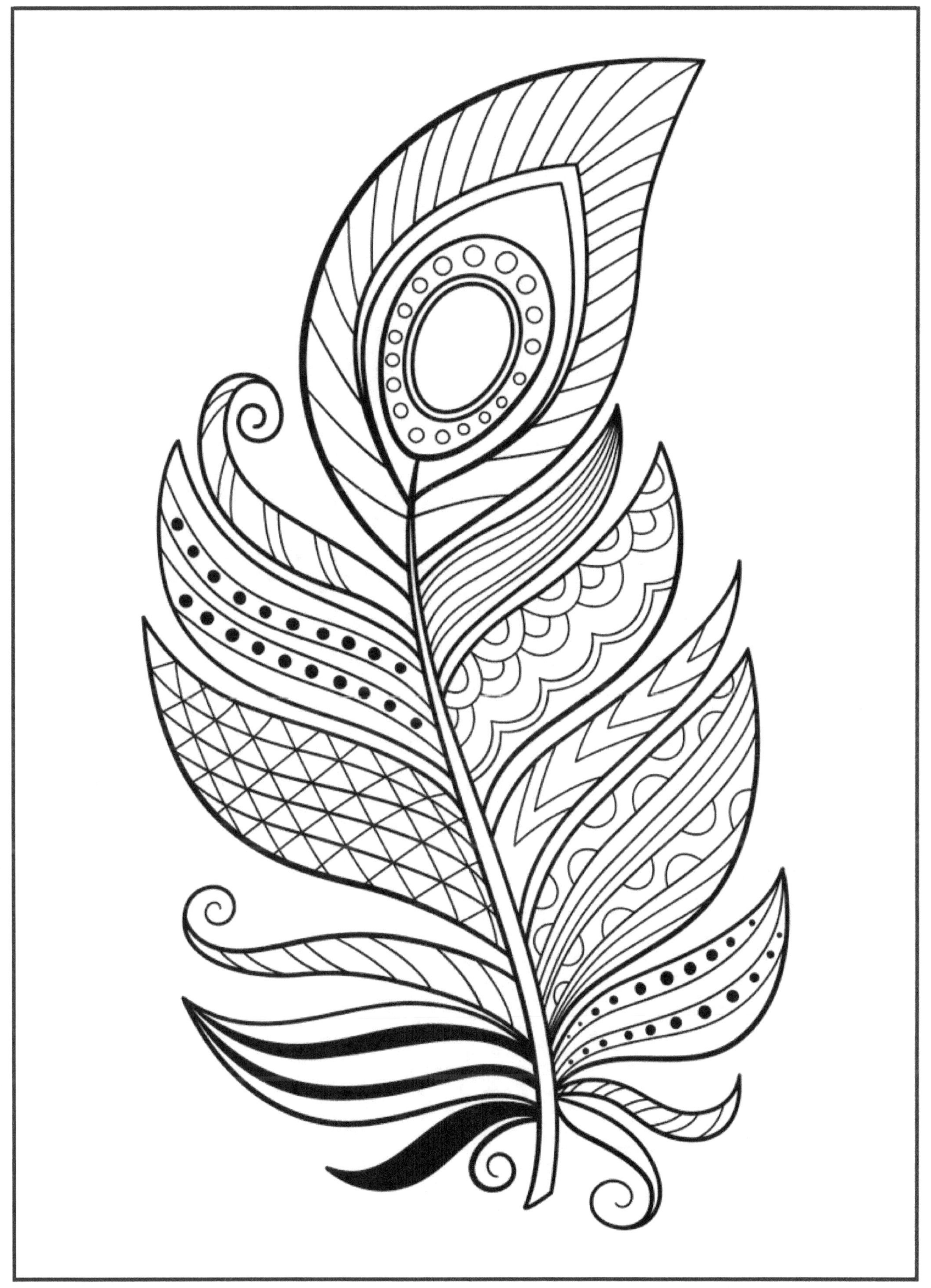

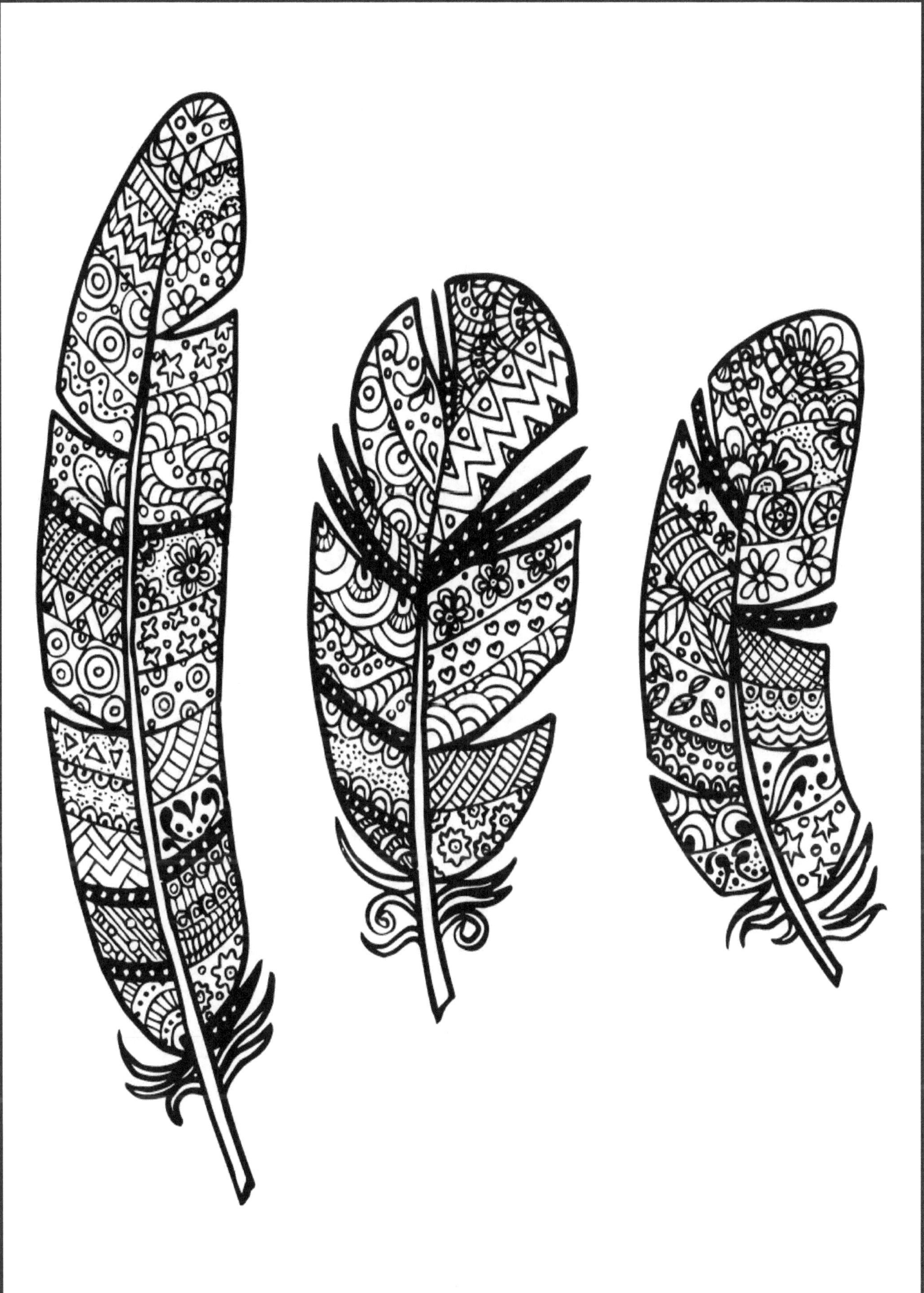

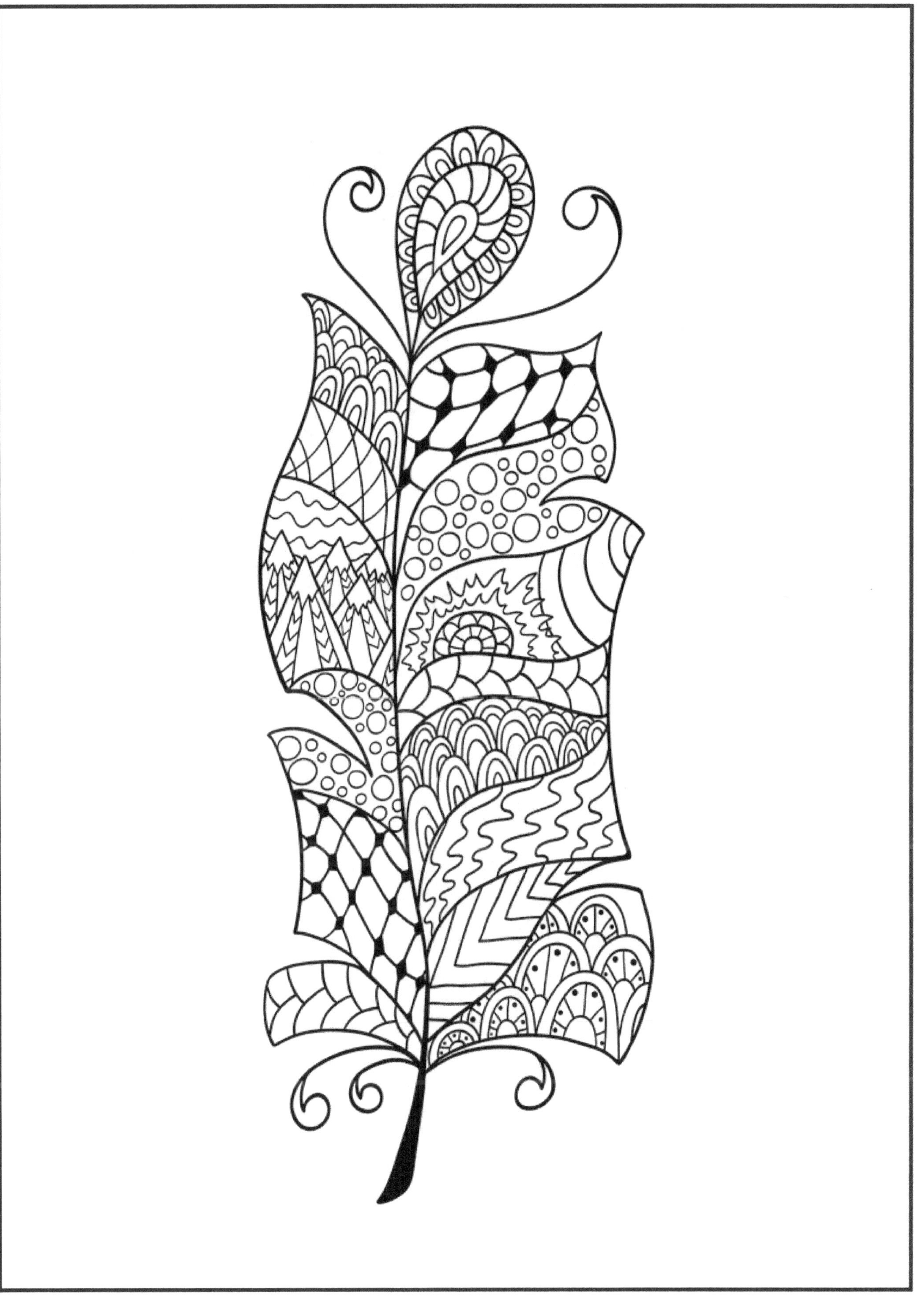

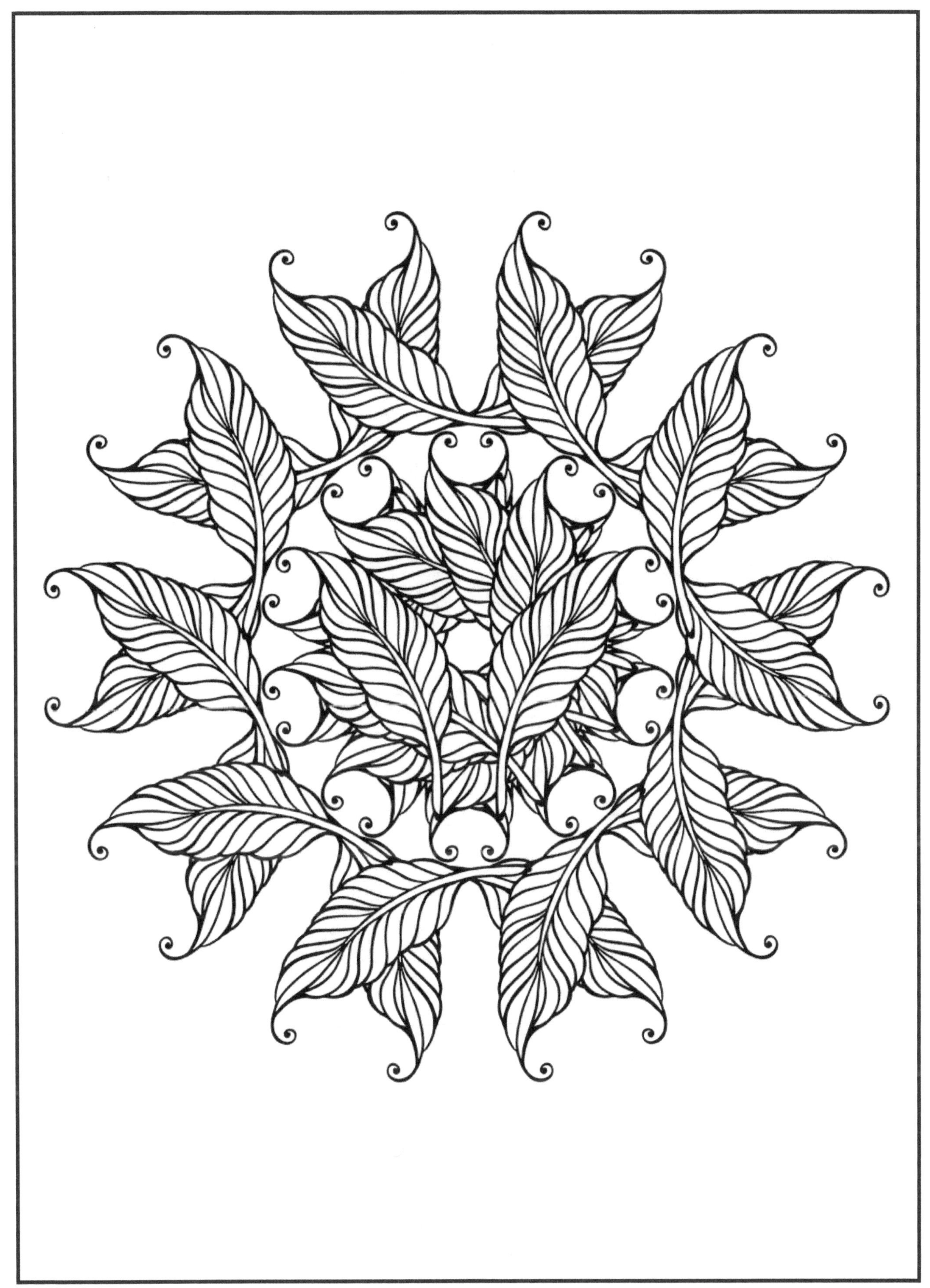

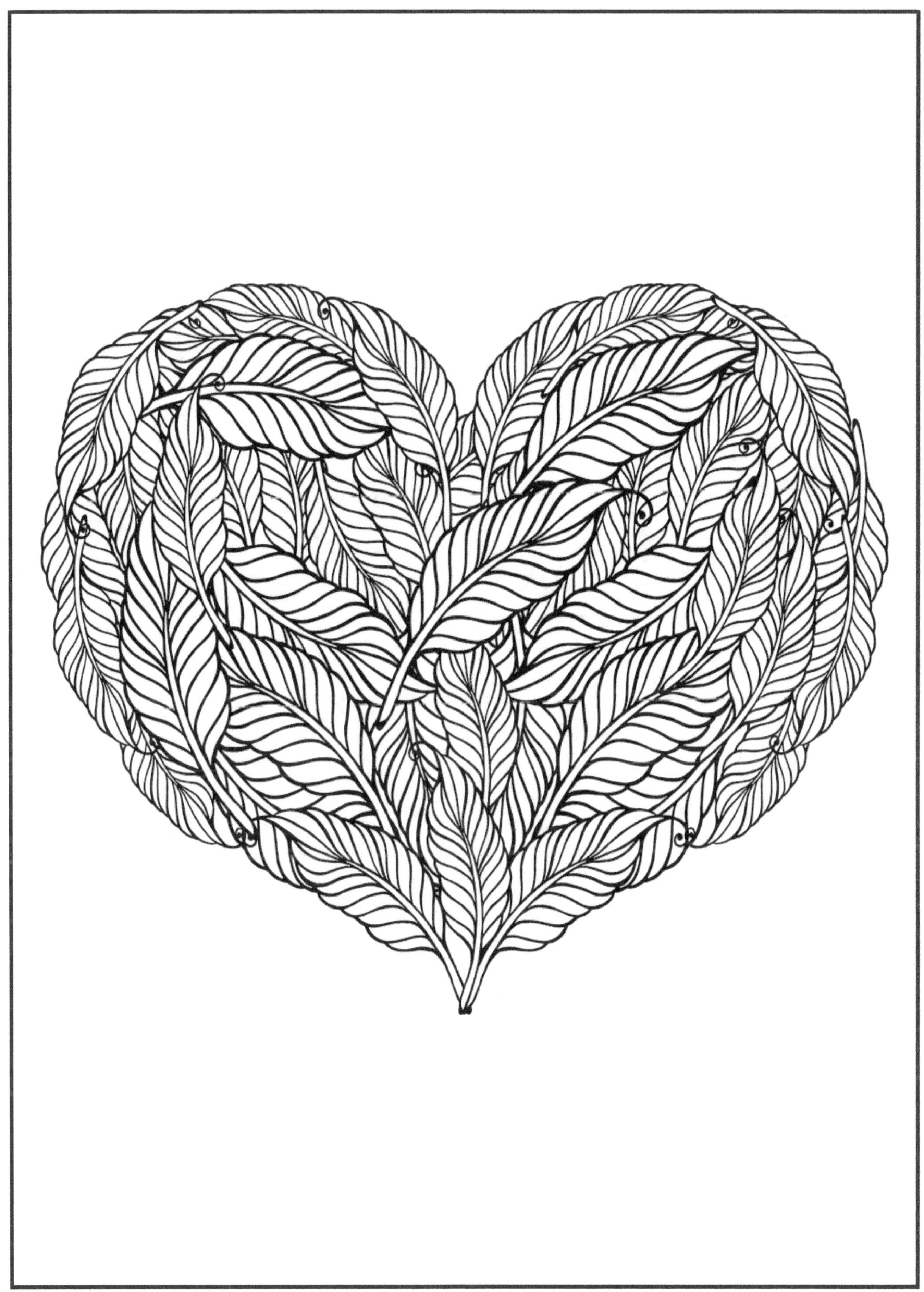

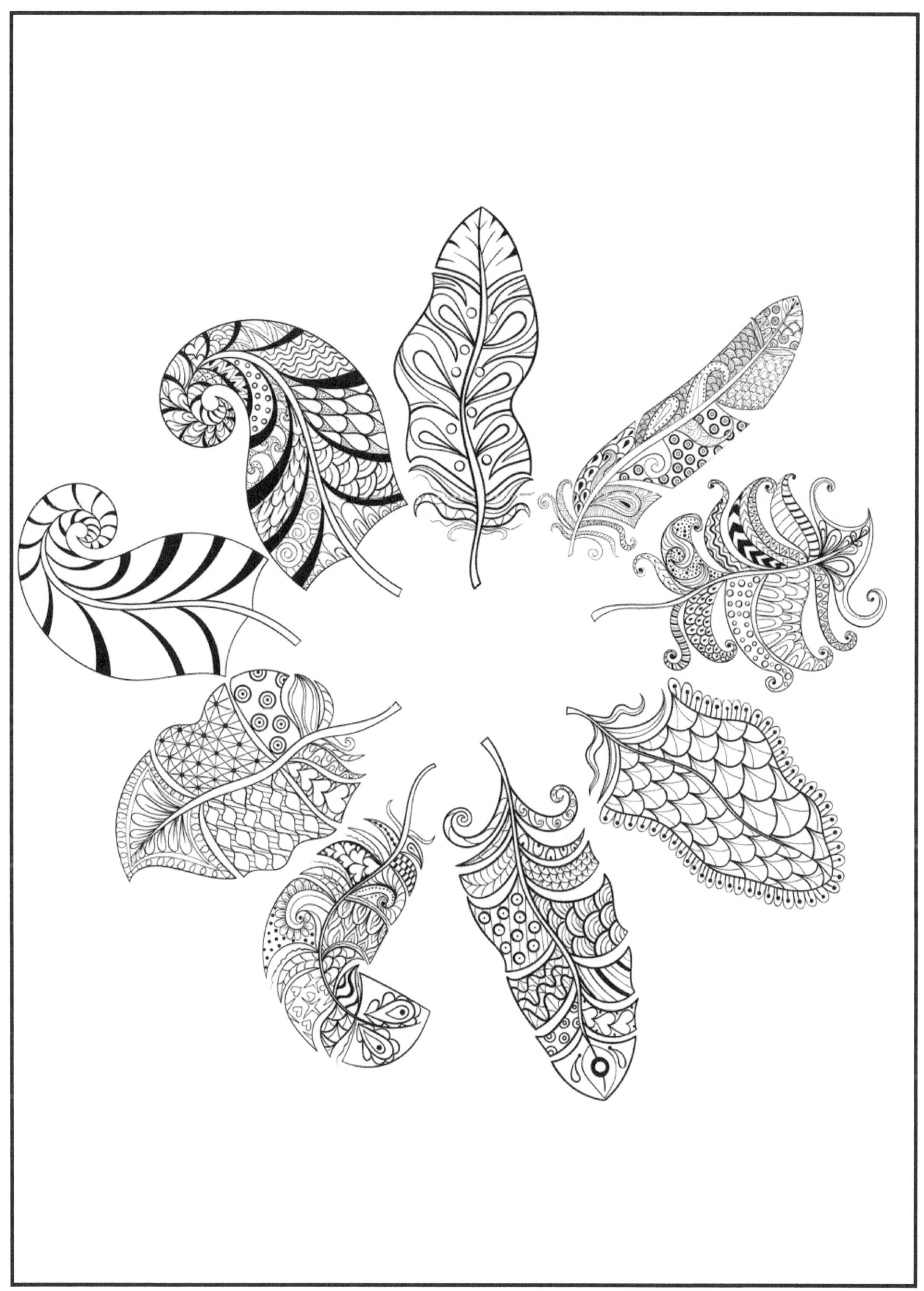

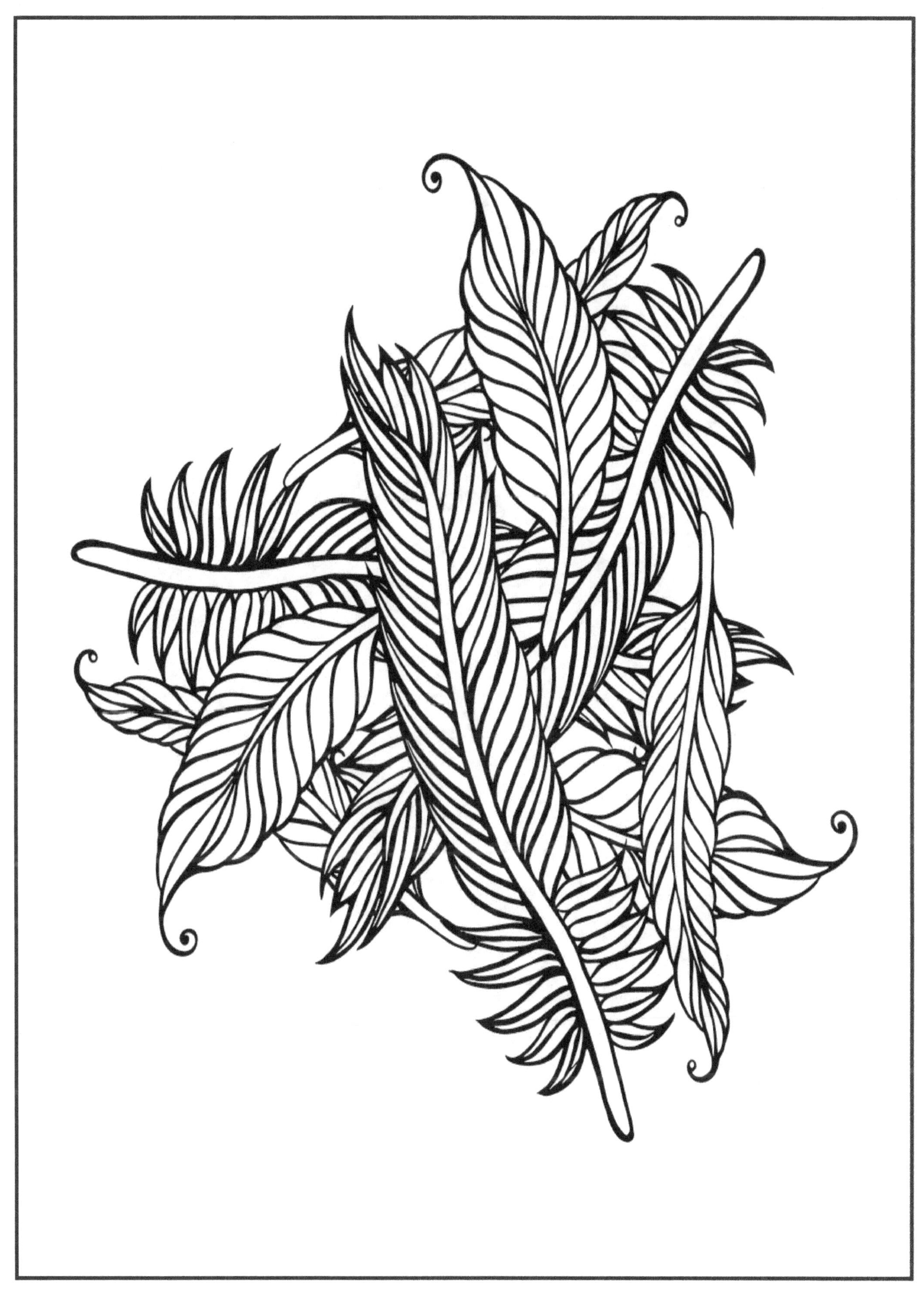

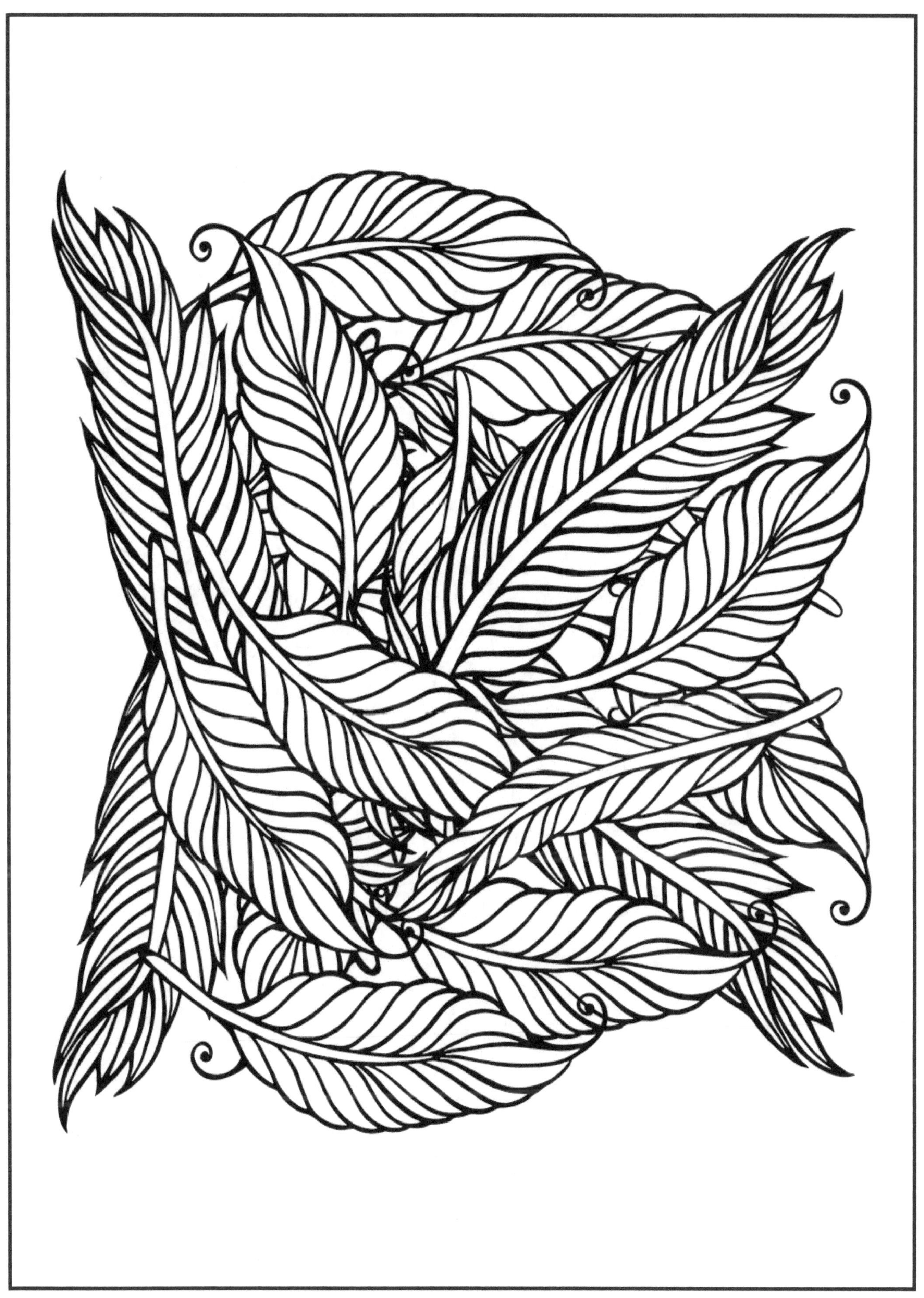

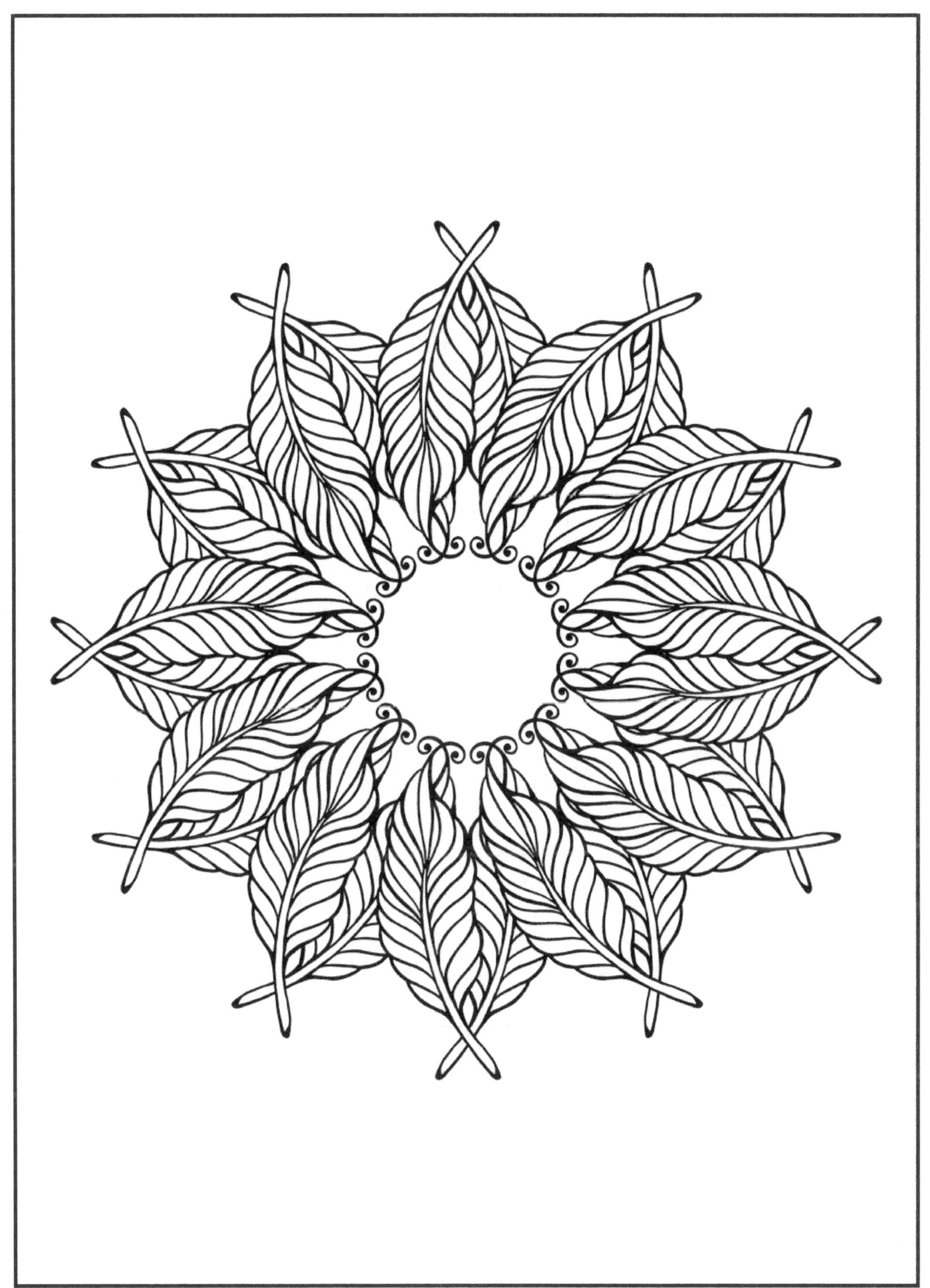

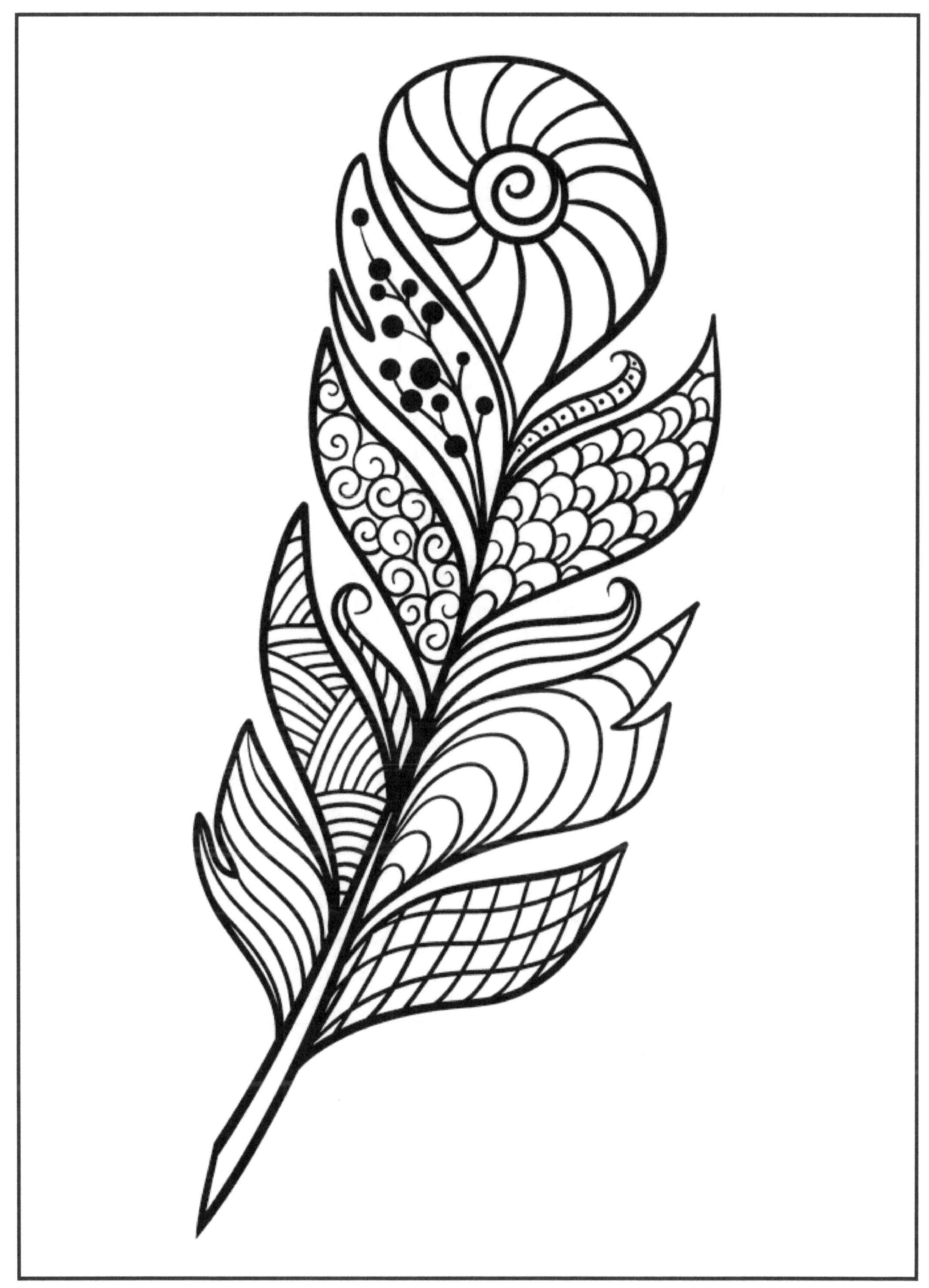

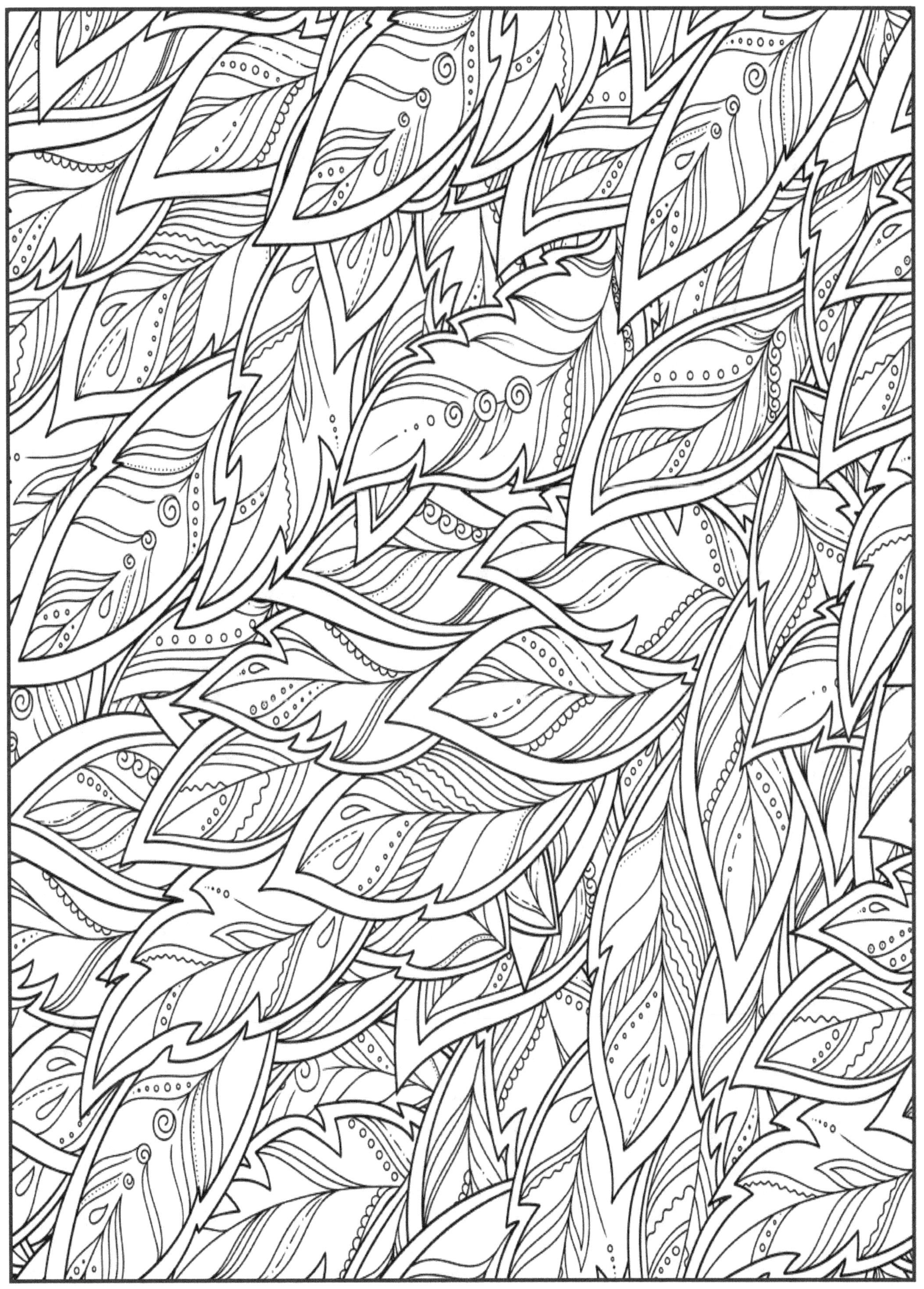

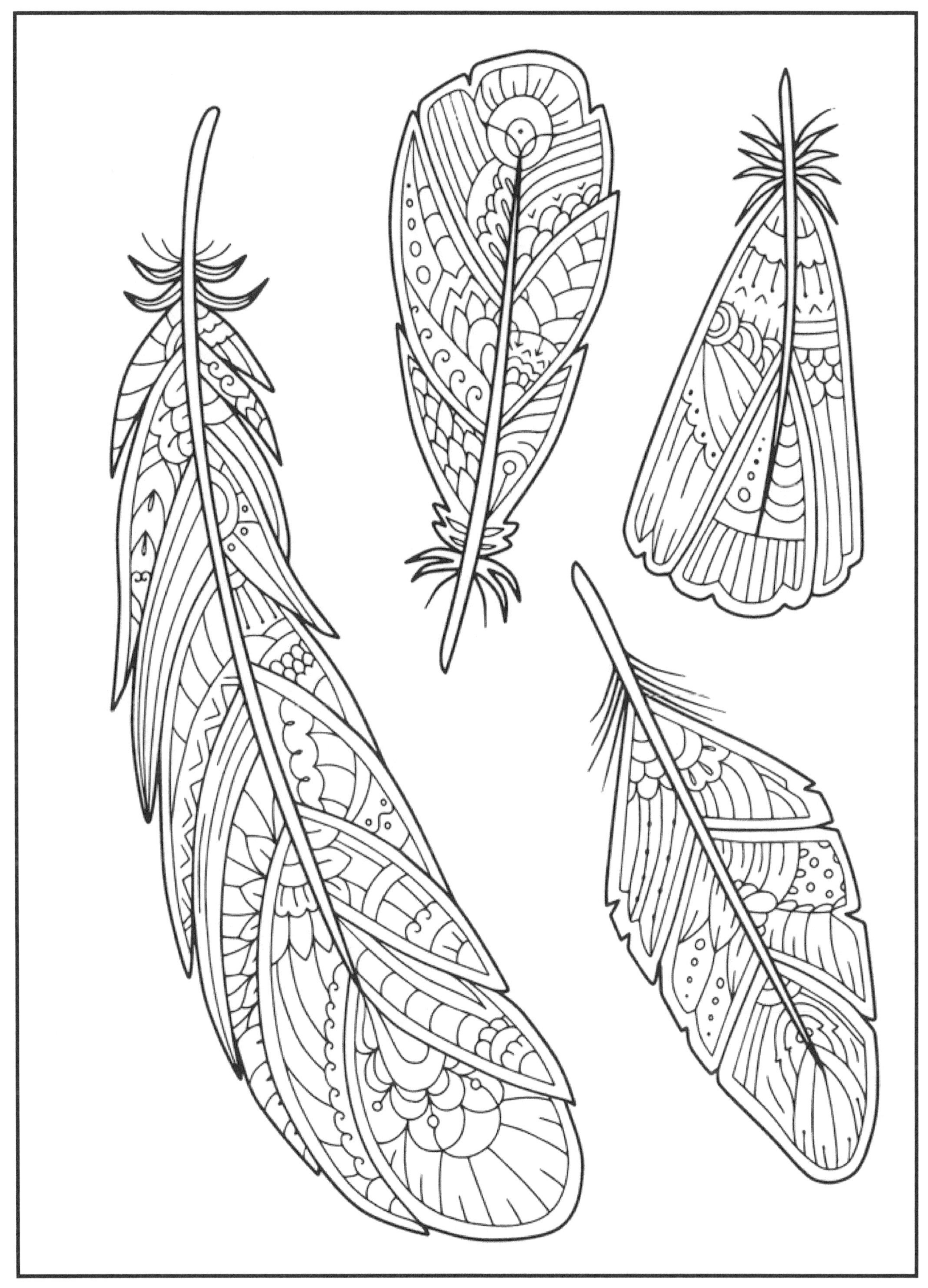

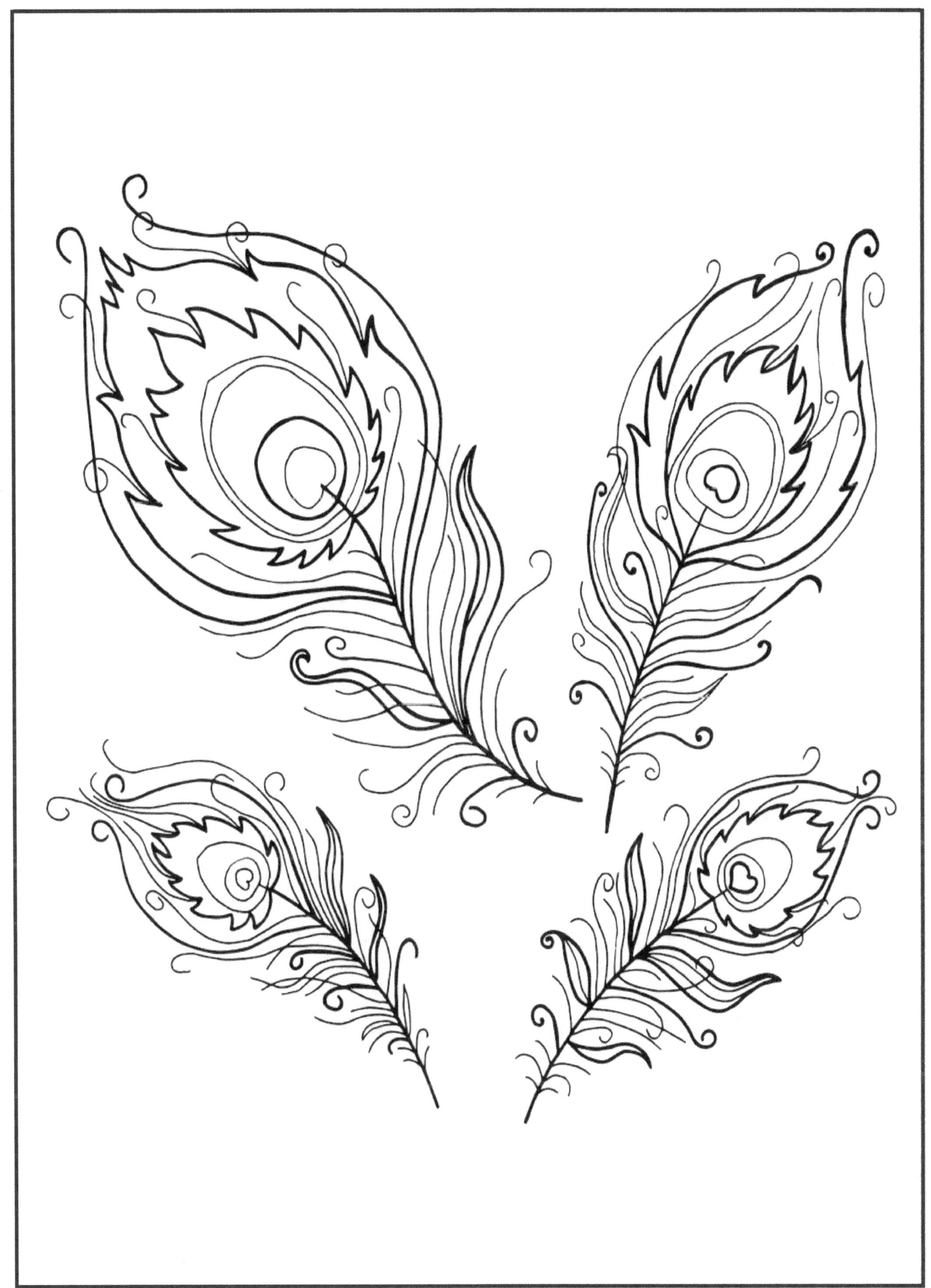

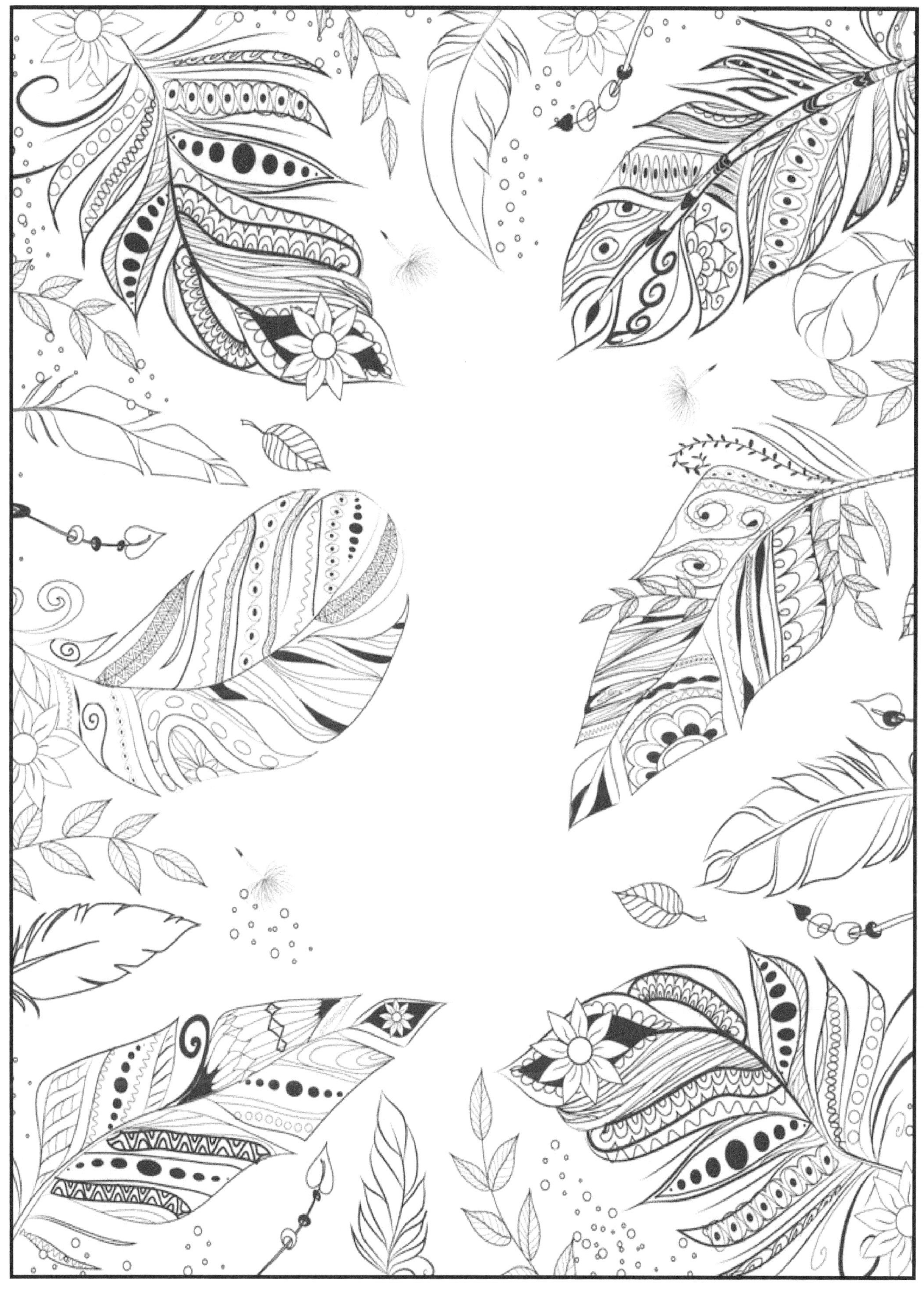

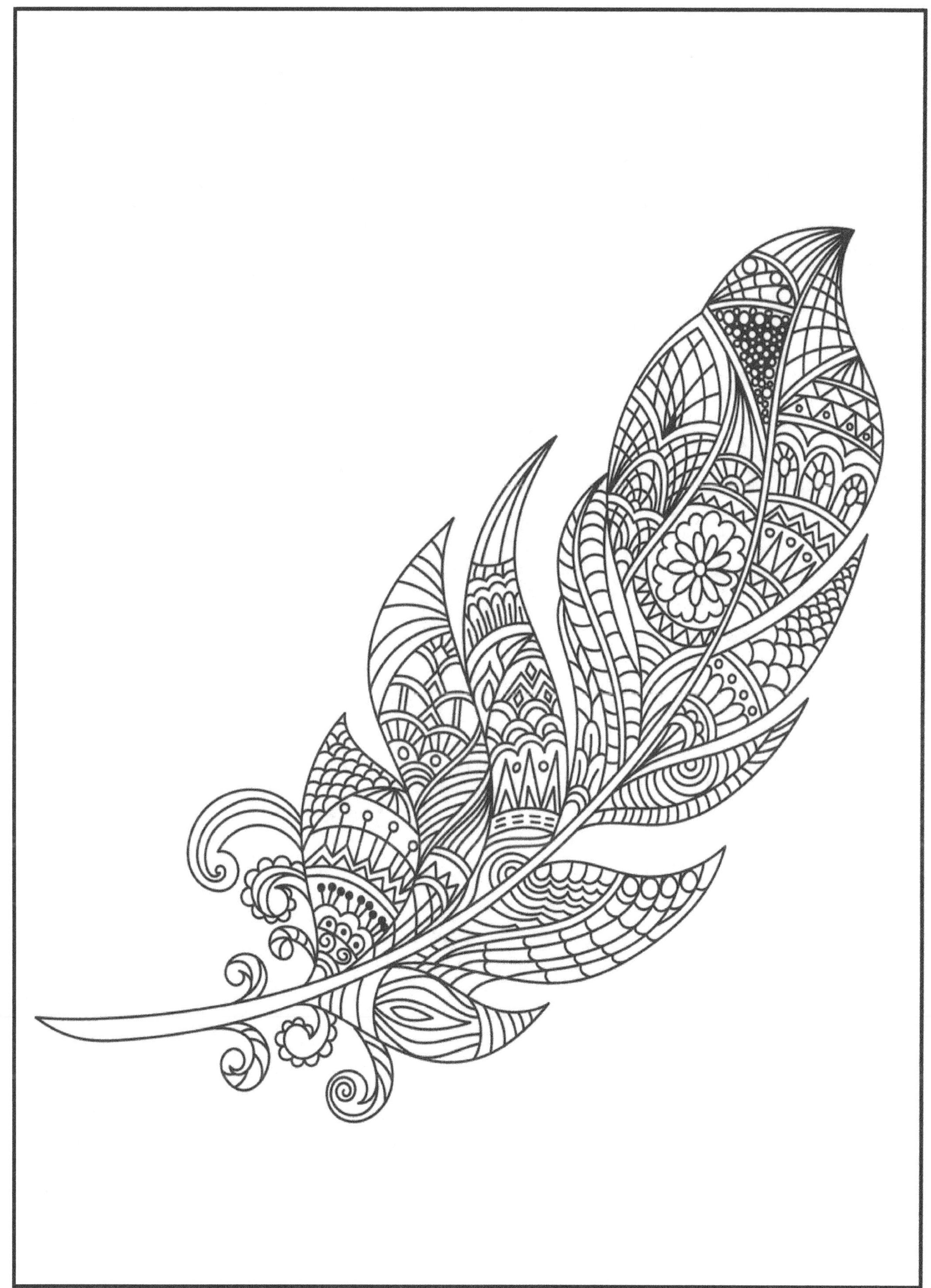

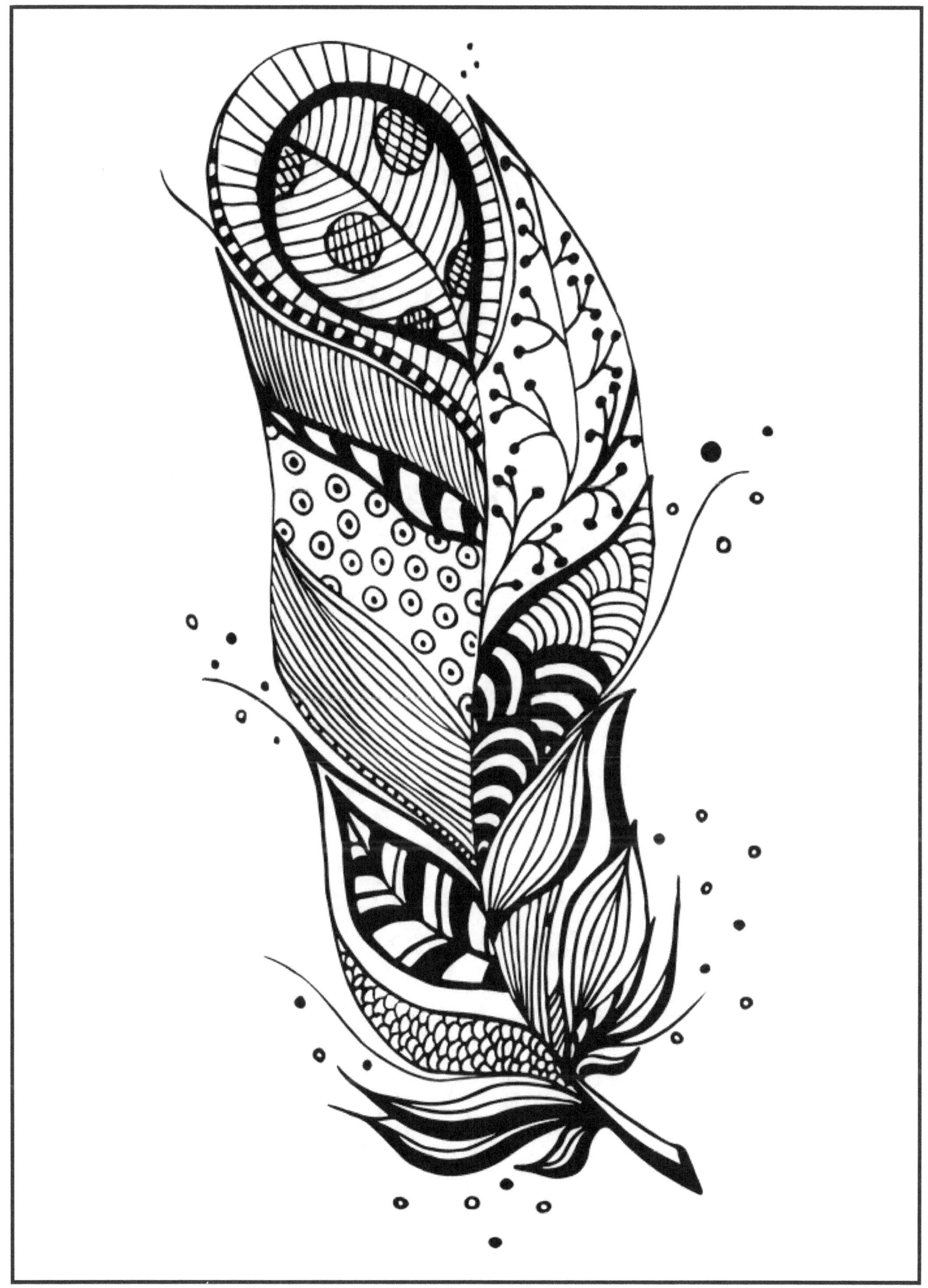

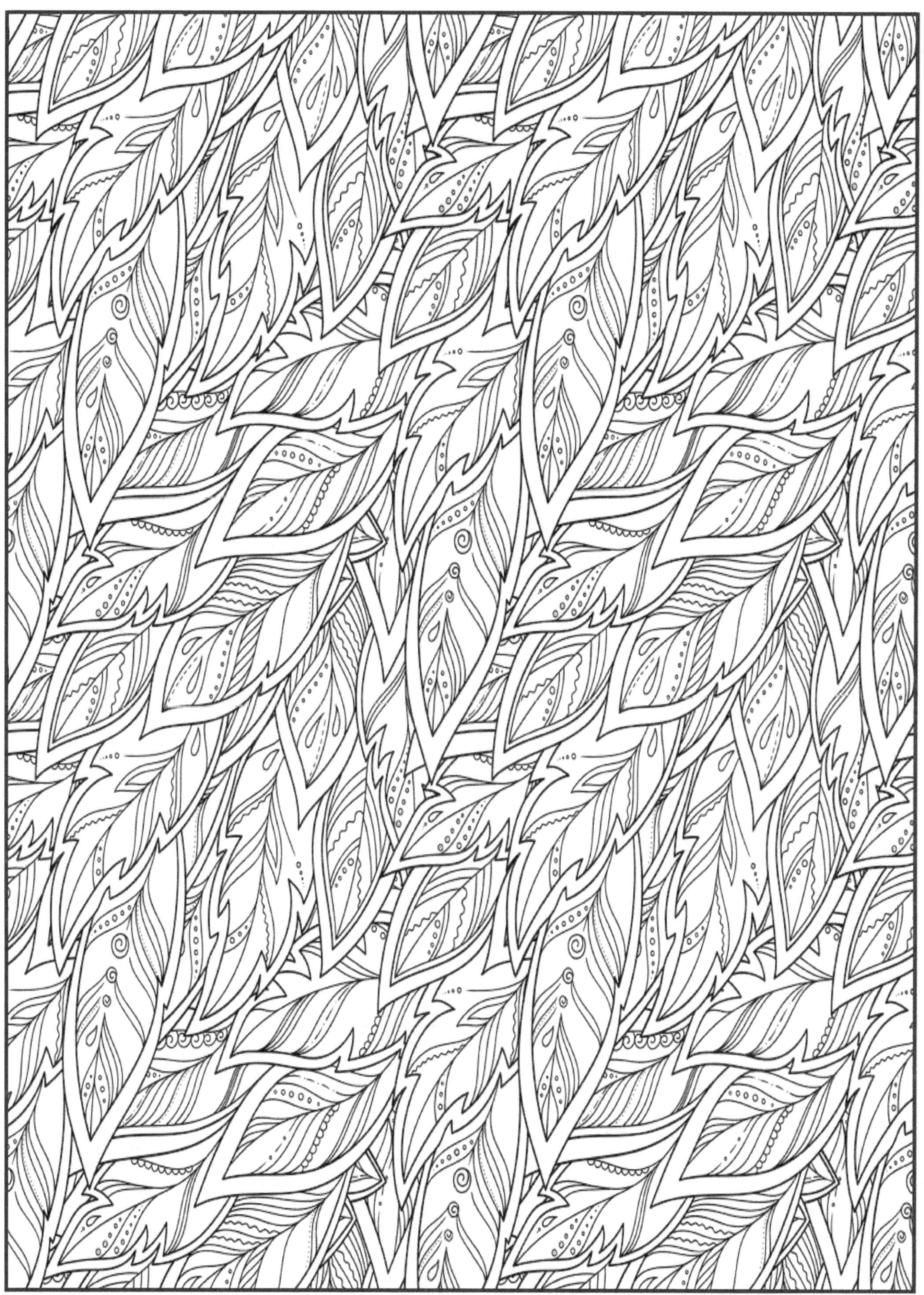

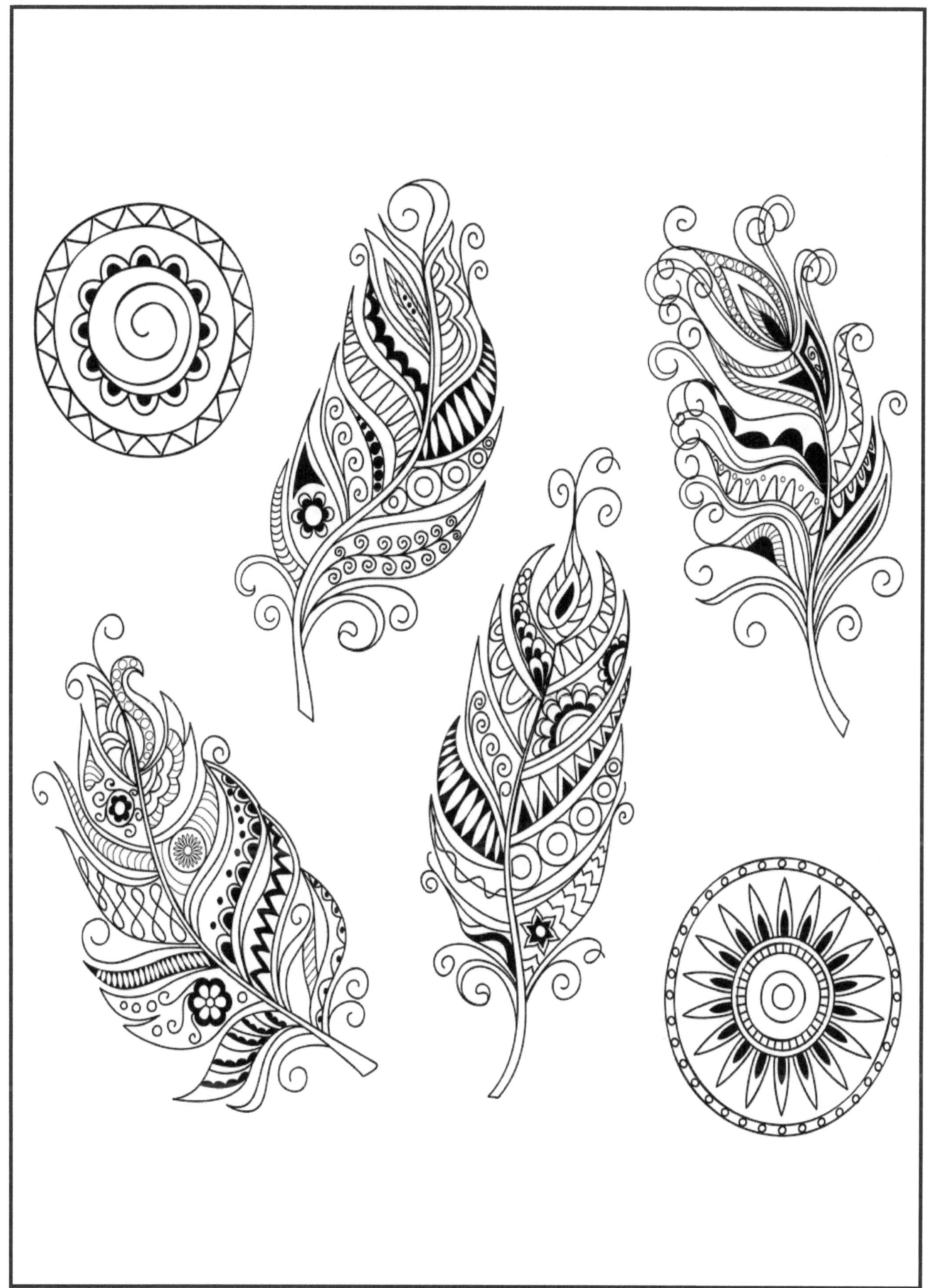

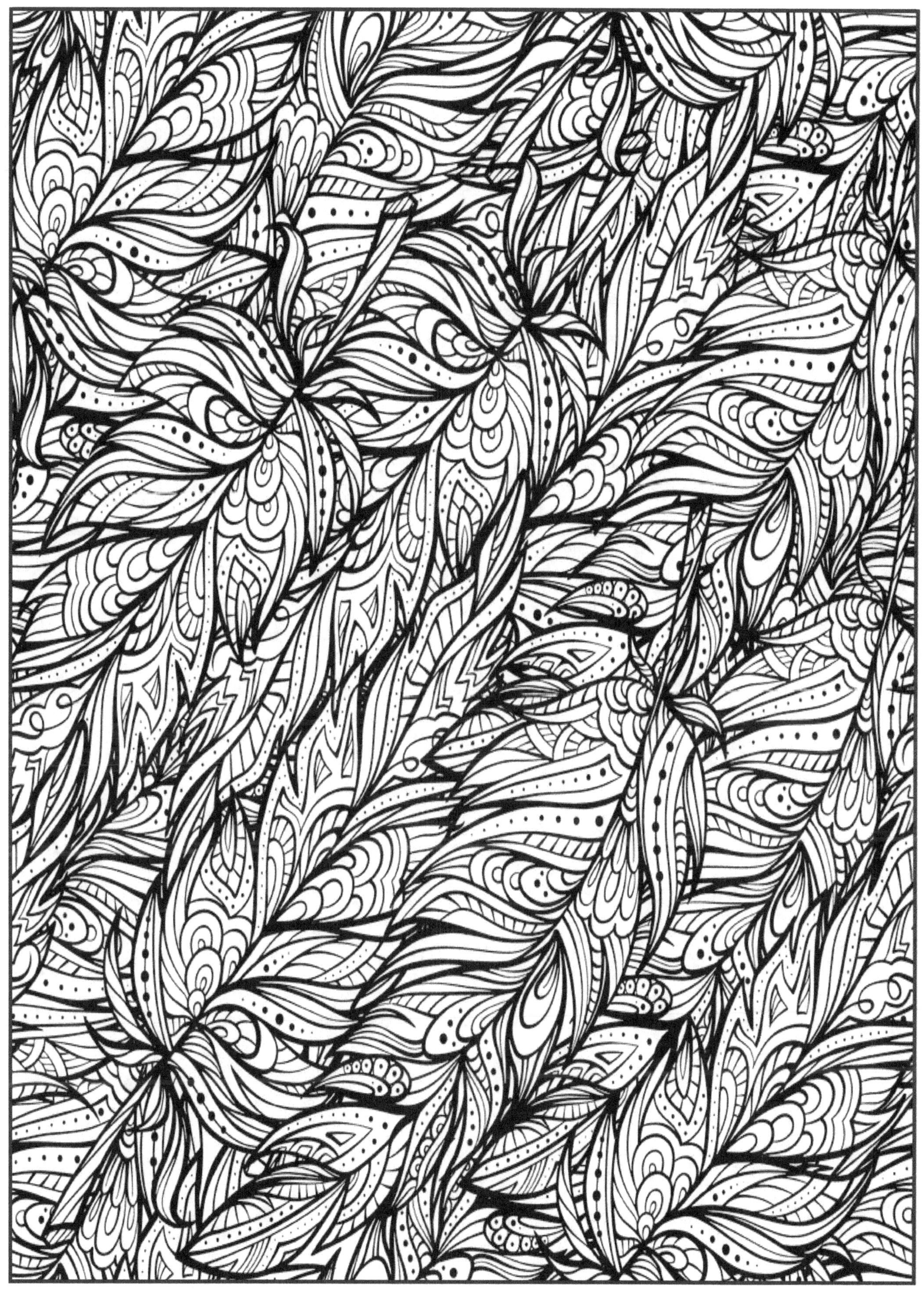

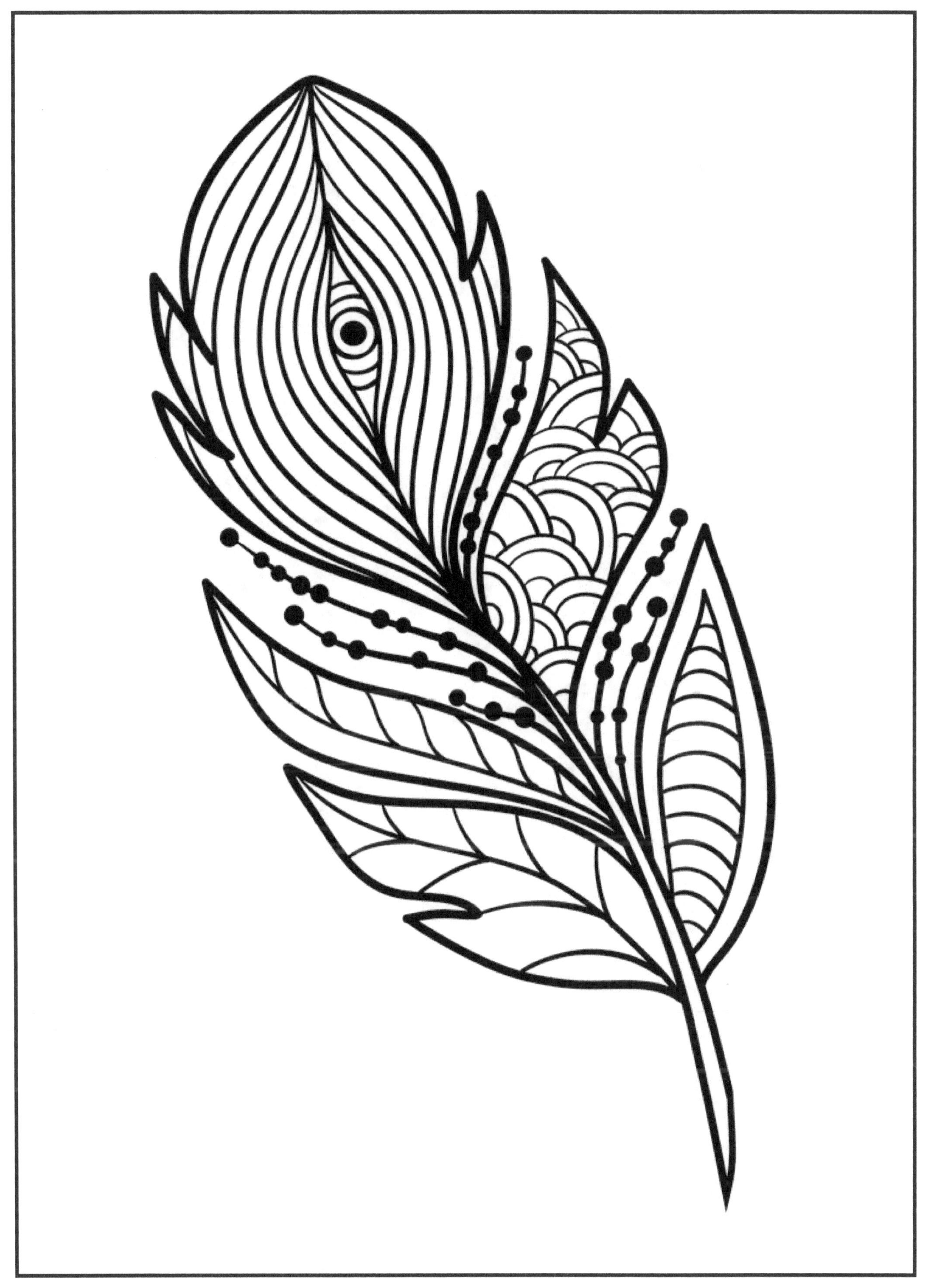

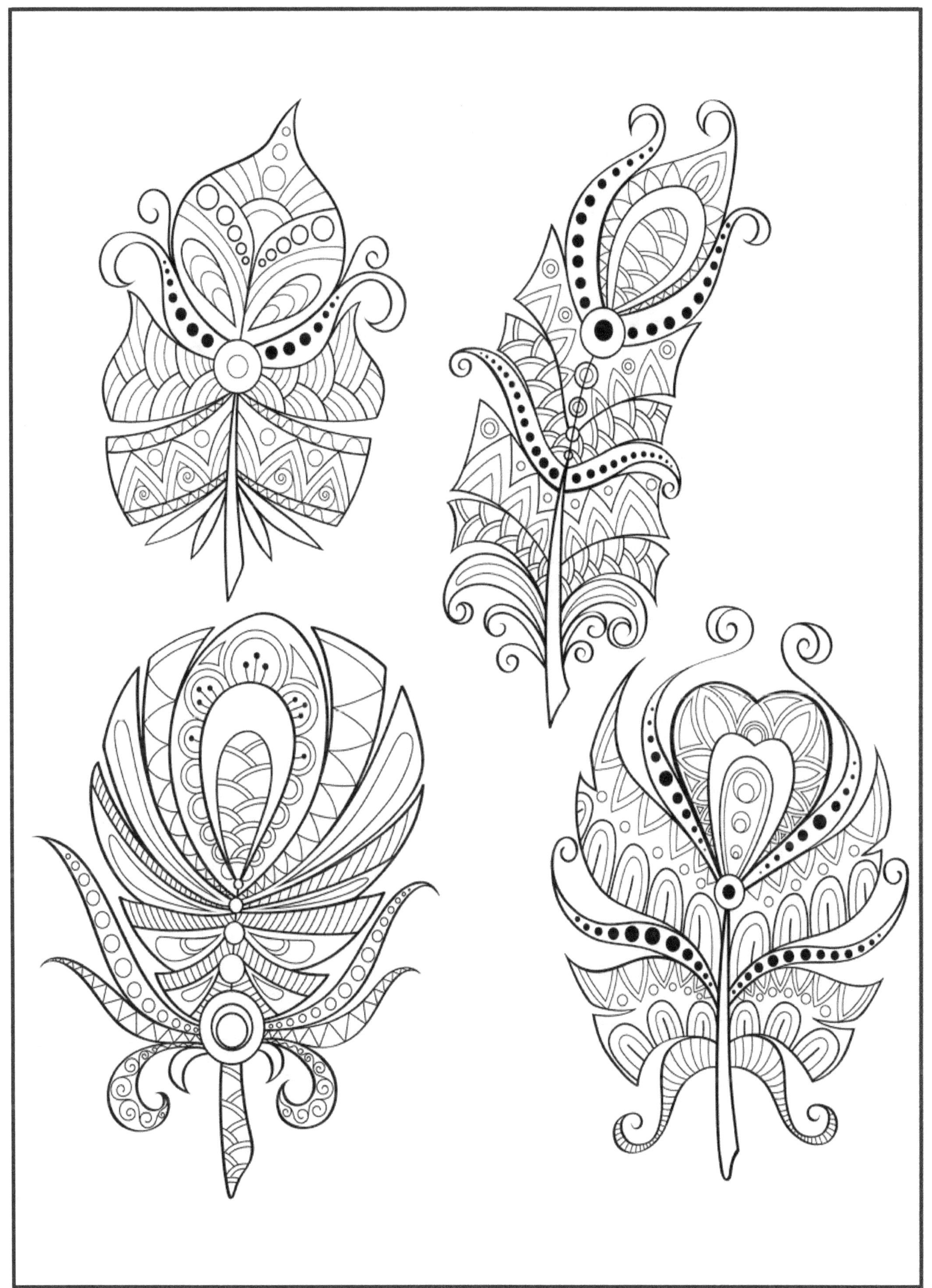

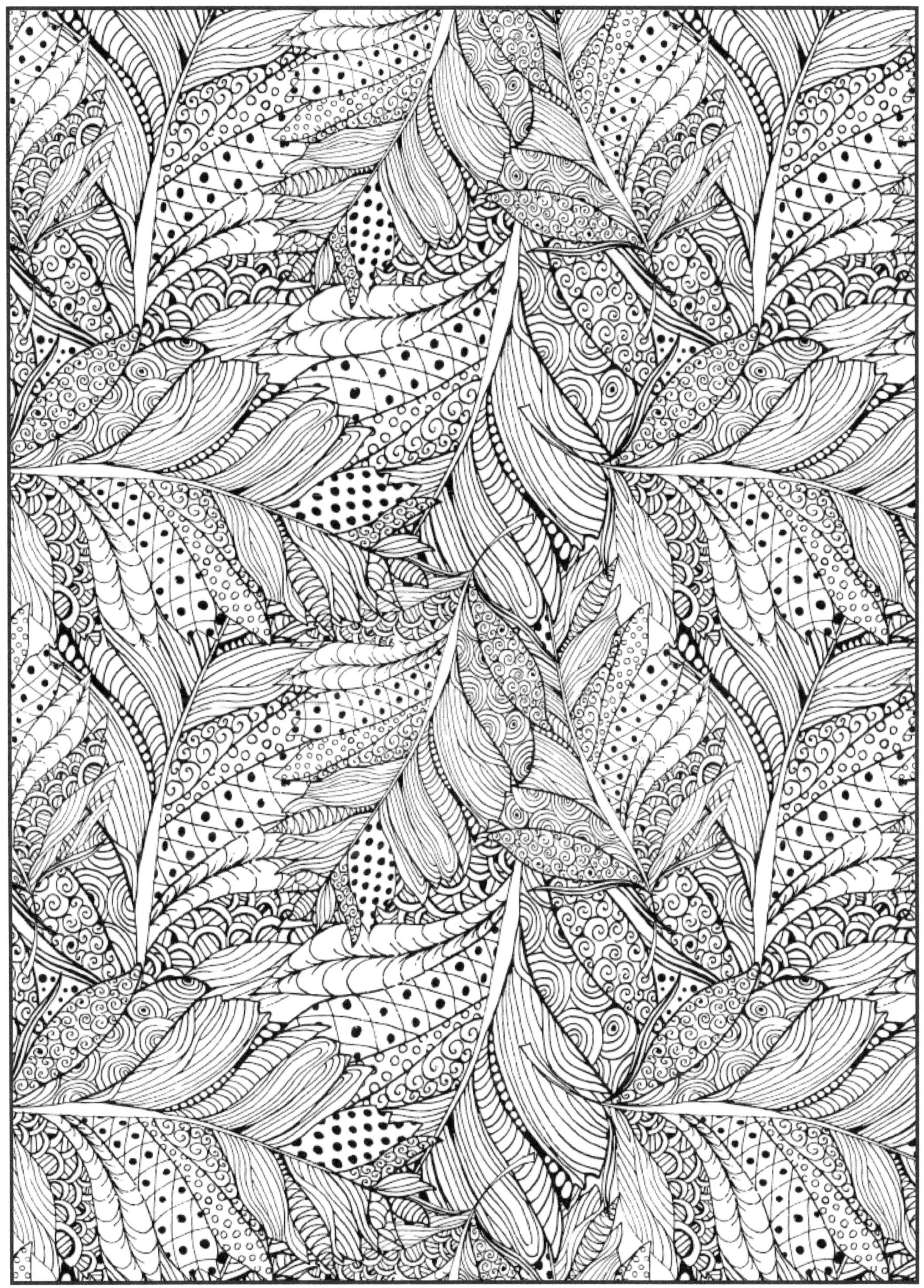

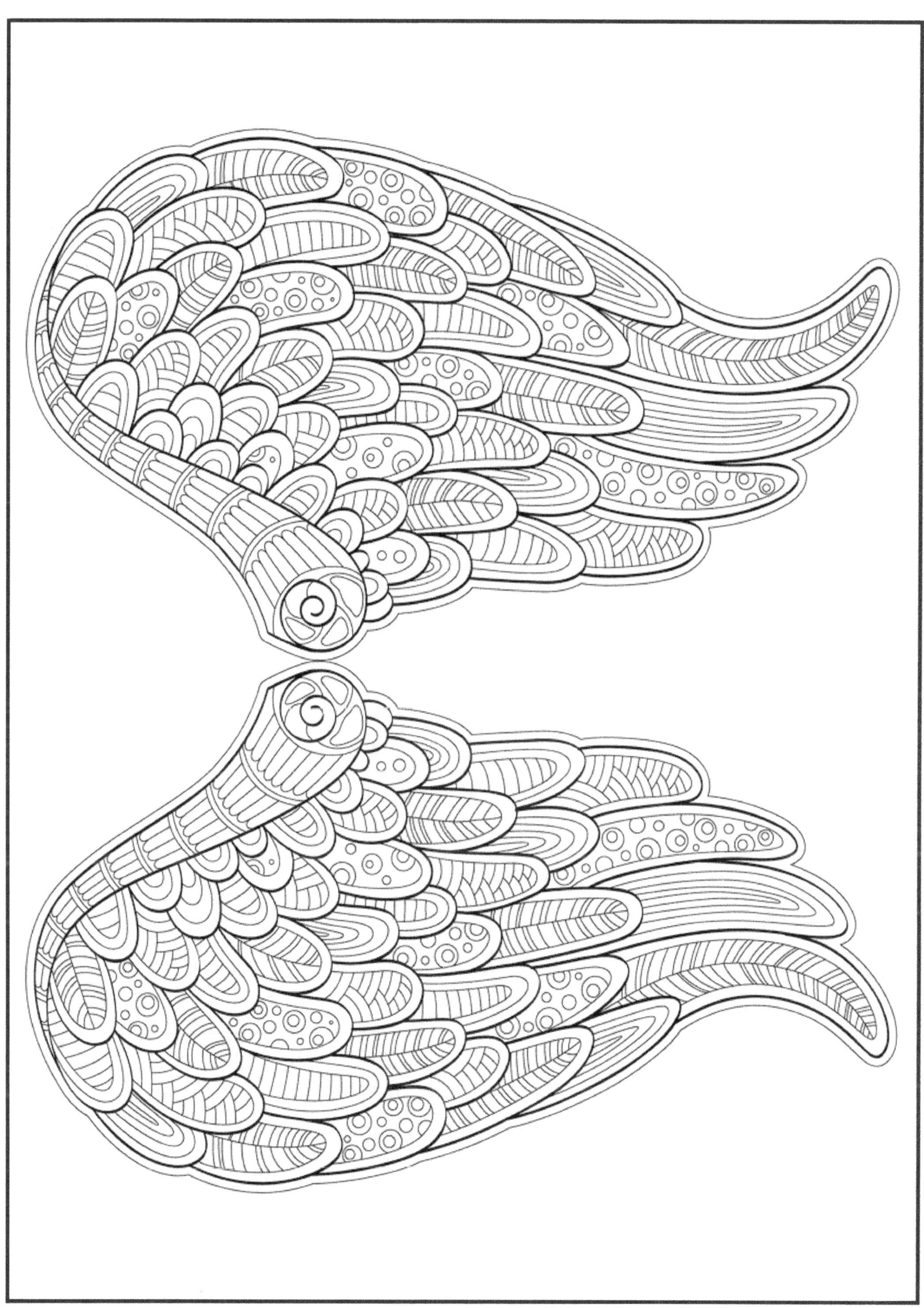

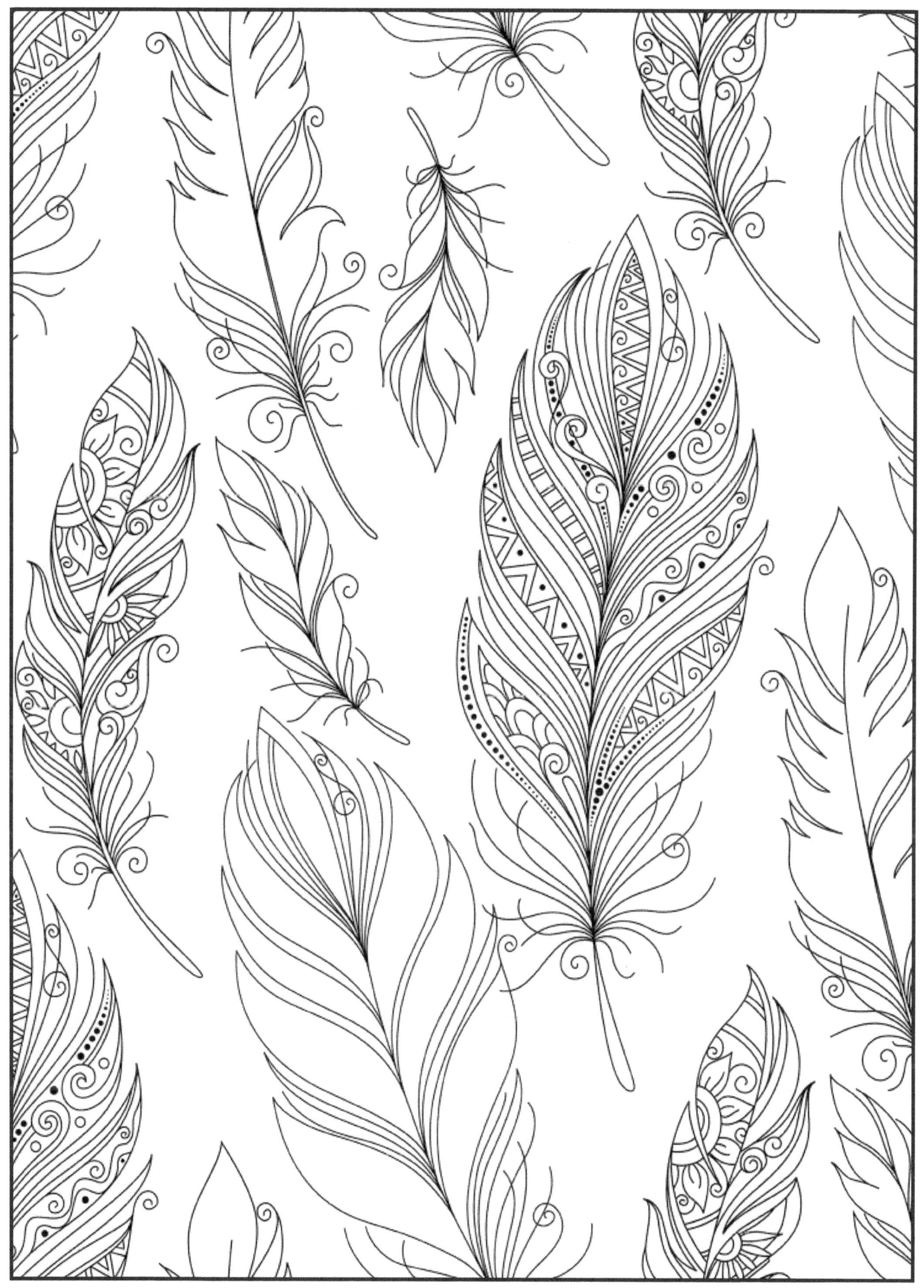

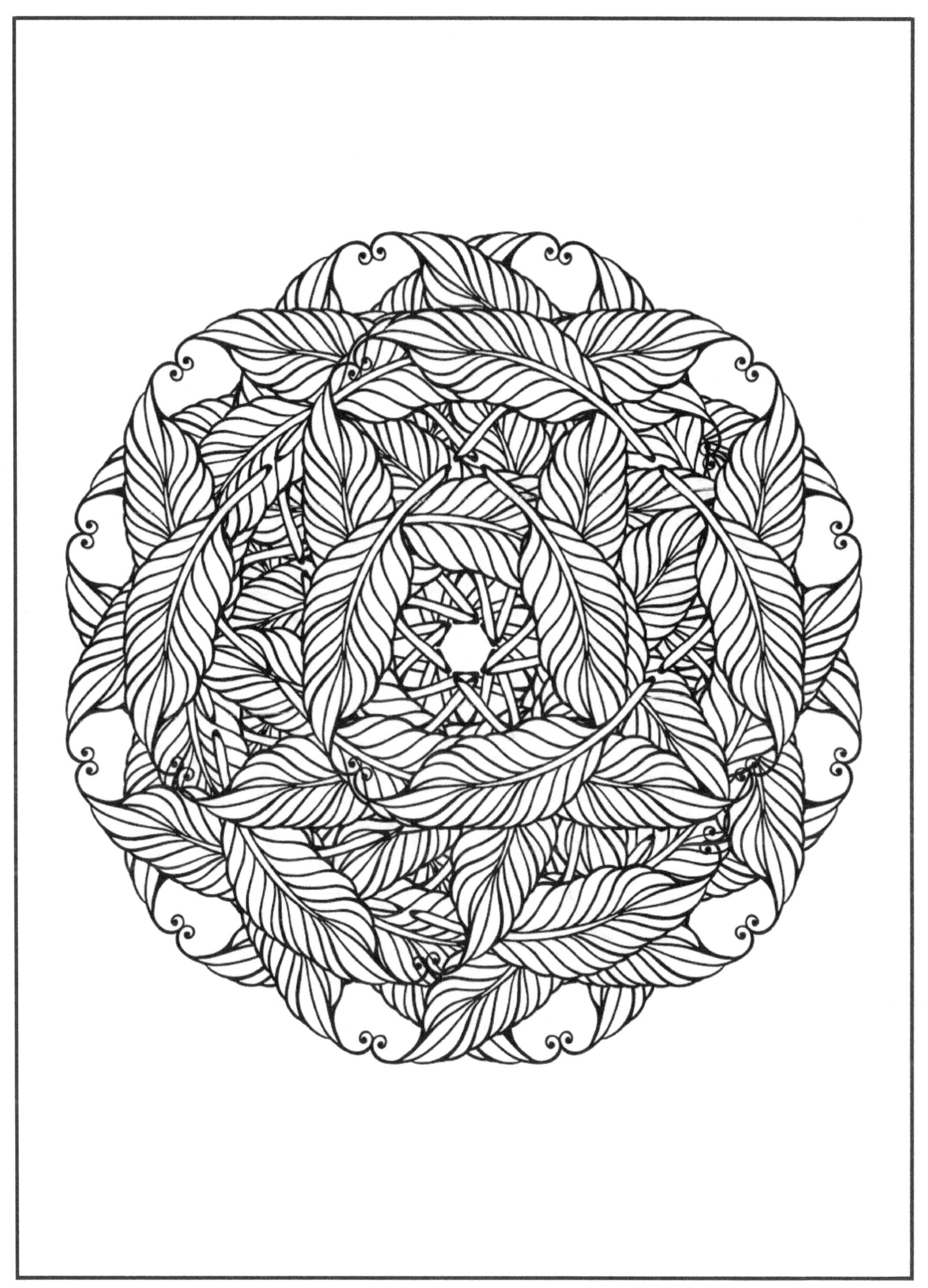

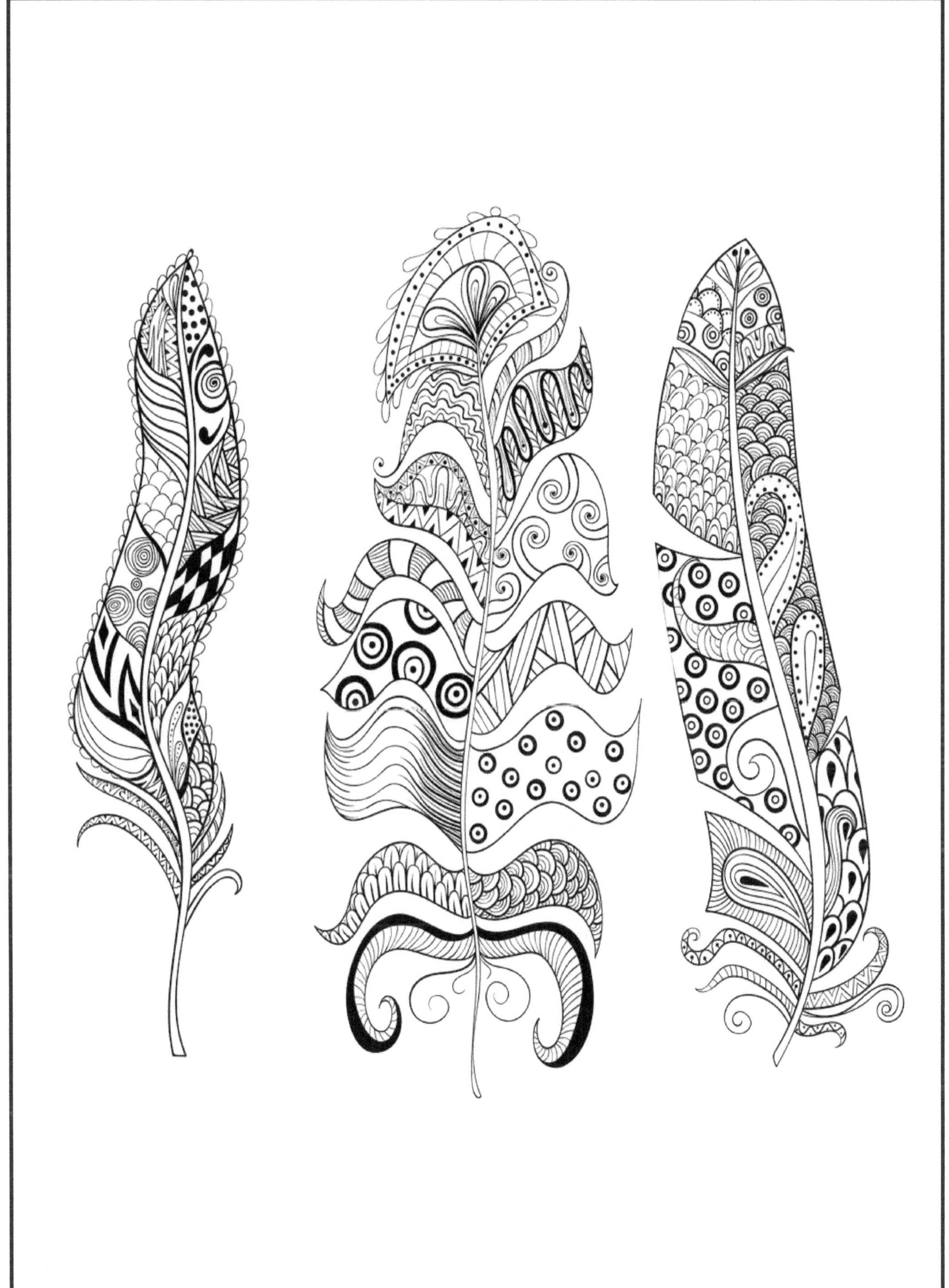

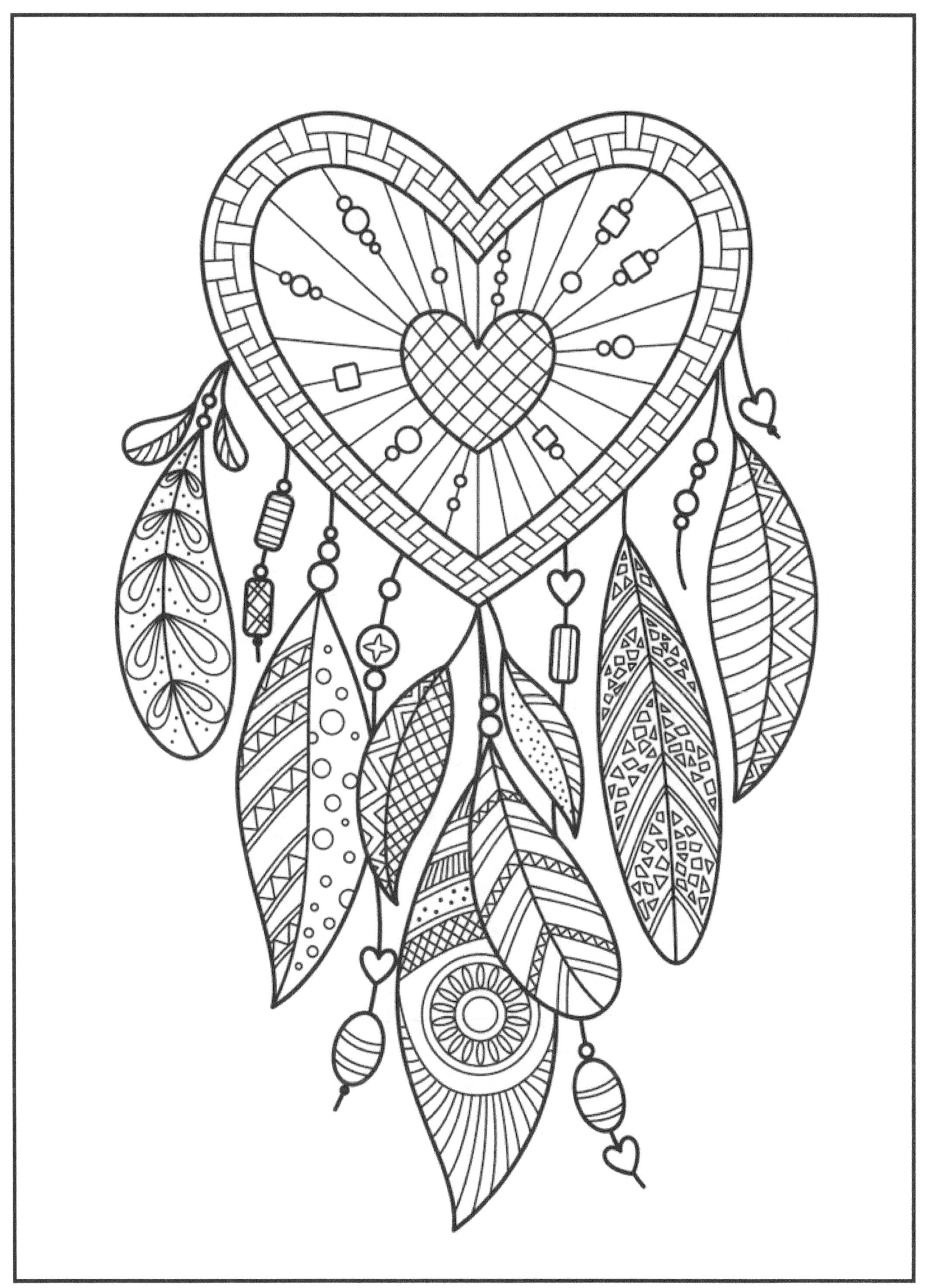

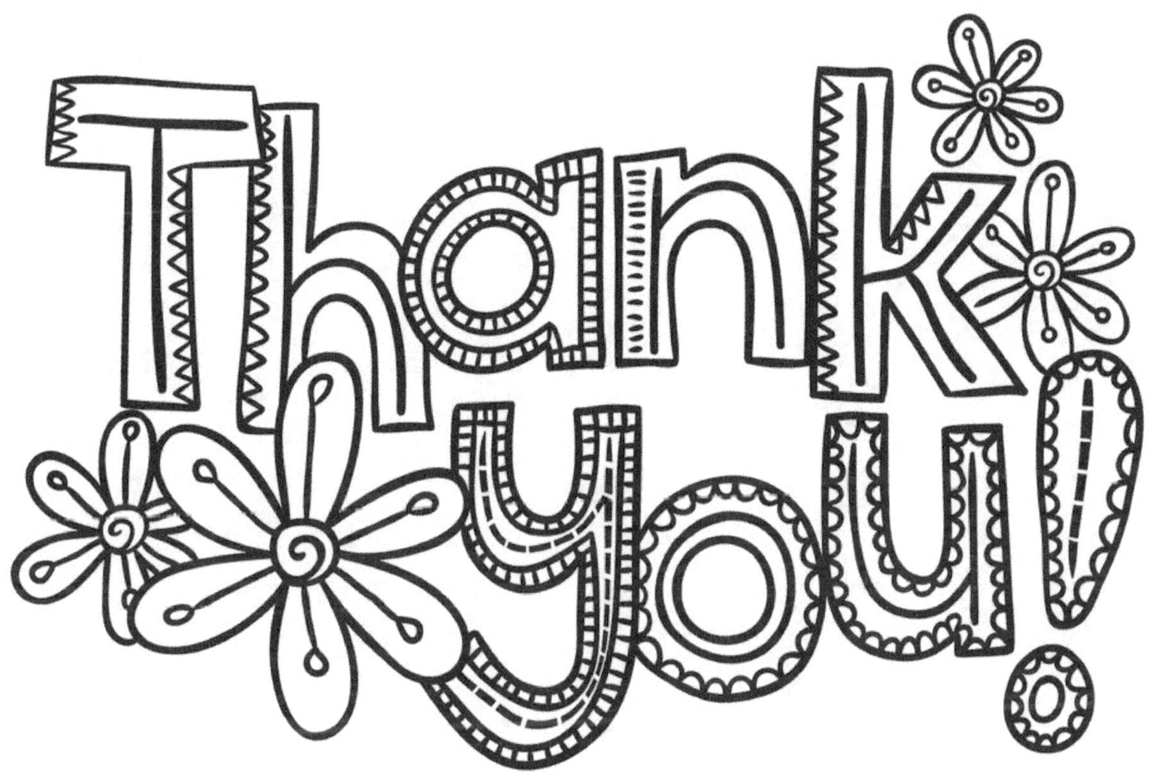

Thank you!